SOUTH WEST BRANCH

D1579957

BITE

WITHDRAWN

Inverclyde Libraries

34106   002745565

BITE

A VAMPIRE HANDBOOK

KEVIN JACKSON

Portobello

Published by Portobello Books Ltd 2009
This paperback edition published 2010

Portobello Books Ltd
12 Addison Avenue
London
W11 4QR

Copyright © Kevin Jackson 2009

The right of Kevin Jackson to be identified as the author of this work has been
asserted by him in accordance with the Copyright, Designs and Patents Act 1988

A CIP catalogue record is available from the British Library

9 8 7 6 5 4 3 2 1

ISBN 978 1 84627 212 7

www.portobellobooks.com

Text designed and typeset in Meridien Roman by Sarah Hodder
Maps designed by Barbara Hilliam

Printed and bound in Great Britain by CPI Bookmarque, Croydon

For Anne Billson and Kim Newman
Princess and Prince of Darkness

CONTENTS

LIST OF MAPS

INTRODUCTION

I was a teenage vampire

At the age of, oh, twelve or thirteen, my career plans were already fully developed. My heart was set on becoming a vampire.

To be exact, I wanted to be a vampire exactly like Christopher Lee in the Hammer films. (I had yet actually to watch one, but I read about them avidly in *Famous Monsters of Filmland*.) Eternal life, snappy clothes, terrific real estate . . . gosh. As puberty advanced, the idea of a trio of eternally youthful Brides started to seem quite a bonus, too. The only disadvantages were that you had to fang some poor fool for dinner once in a while, and keep an eye out for meddlesome Dutchmen armed with wooden stakes. It sounded a lot more interesting than accountancy.

Most men who enjoy vampire films and fiction have felt something of this singular attraction. All our other mass-cultural monsters are uncouth or ghastly. Werewolves? Hairy, noisy, slobbering brutes with indiscriminate appetites: an obvious metaphor for adolescent boys. The Frankenstein monster? Ugly, dim-witted, poor fashion sense. Zombies? Smelly, sluggish, brain-dead creatures ruled by herd instincts – an obvious metaphor for lecturers in cultural studies. Robots? Toasters with attitude. Ghosts? No substance. Godzilla? A newt on steroids.

No, only vampires were suave, elegant, erudite and even witty. Their bodies were cool, and their style was cooler. Sign me up. Nor, by the way, was it only the chaps of my generation who felt this way.

In her thoughtful study *Our Vampires, Ourselves,* Nina Auerbach explains how, as a girl growing up in the strait-laced America of the 1950s, the fantasy of being vampires kept her and her friends from dying of suburban conformity and boredom. 'Trying to make us popular,' she writes, 'our worried parents forced us away from Transylvania to dances and parties, where we spent most of the evening making vampire faces at each other . . .' Vampires helped the ostracized, unpopular Nina grow up into Professor Auerbach, famous author, noted feminist. 'Vampires were supposed to menace women, but to me at least, they promised protection against a destiny of girdles, spike heels, and approval.'

The common note here is escape: escape from boredom into fascination, loneliness into power, everyday tedium into timeless myth. In my case, this particular escape route gave way to others. I read Steinbeck and wanted to become a marine biologist; T. E. Lawrence, and wanted to become a guerrilla fighter; André Breton, and wanted to become a Surrealist. But early ambitions always leave their mark, and I continued to find Dracula and his kind hard to resist. Every so often I would sneak off into darkened rooms and feast greedily on sanguinary images. And the vampire army was obviously doing just fine without me in the ranks, swelling in numbers and influence year by year, until now, in the early twenty-first century, we are in the midst of a vampire craze as large and as lucrative as any the world has known since the 1820s; in fact, a great deal larger. It is no surprise to me that so many girls are now thrilled by the *Twilight* books and film; I clearly remember the allure of the darkness, and the freedoms to be found there.

To be sure, there are other, non-escapist reasons to be drawn to vampires; the undead have been asked or made to stand for capitalist tyranny (see Marx), communist tyranny (see modern Romania), Romantic rebellion, the 'return of the repressed' (see Freud and epigones), drug addiction, sexually transmitted diseases in general and HIV/Aids in particular, homosexuality, social Darwinism, necrophilia . . . But the vampire metaphor, though protean, is not all-embracing. Always at the core is the night-walker, the bloodsucker, the doomed immortal. Anyone who has ever experienced the delicious shudder that comes of encountering this dark archangel will understand why the mythology, like the creature itself, will never truly die.

K. J.
Maine, March 2009

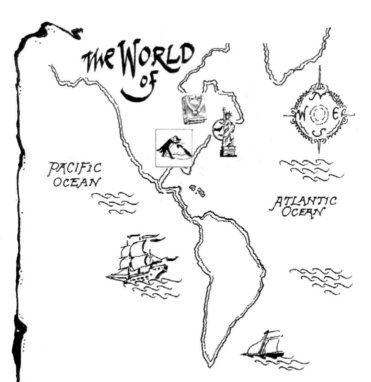

THE WORLD OF

PACIFIC OCEAN

ATLANTIC OCEAN

 Romania. The modern state incorporates all of Dracula's familiar turf: Transylvania, Wallachia, the Carpathians, and 'Dracula's Castle'.

 Paris. Home of the great theatrical vampire craze of the 1820s onwards, as recorded by literary historians, and popularized by Anne Rice's 'Interview with the Vampire'. Also home to the vampire-crazy Surrealists.

 New Orleans. Anne Rice territory, of course; but also the site of many subsequent vampire fictions and movies (for example, 'Dracula 2000').

 New York. Setting of 'Nadja', 'The Addiction', 'The Hunger', 'A Vampire in Brooklyn', 'Vampire's Kiss' . . . and many novels.

 Forks, Washington. The setting for Stephanie Meyer's 'Twilight' series. The local economy has already felt the benefit of Meyer pilgrimages.

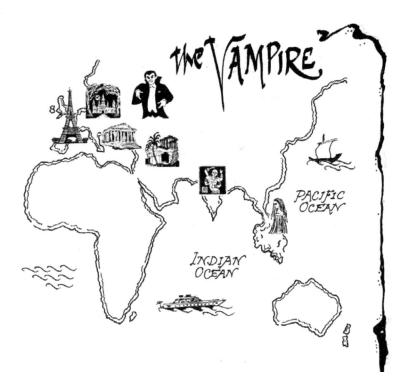

The VAMPIRE

 Hungary. Birthplace of Bela Lugosi and the site of some of 'Dracula's action (Harker recuperates in Budapest). Also, the region most afflicted during the Vampire Epidemics.

 Greece. Home of the classic 'lamia' and the modern 'vrykolakas', among other vampires. According to some authorities, the country where it all began.

 India. The subcontinent teems with dozens, possibly hundreds, of different vampire subspecies.

 Malaysia. A healthy rival to India for sheer variety of vampiric manifestations.

 Iraq. The modern nation which occupies the former territory of Babylon, from which we derive our earliest drawings of vampires.

ONE

VAMPIRE LORE AND GORE

In which we consider quaint, curious and forgotten myths,
legends and rumours

Written reports of the vampire go back to the very earliest civilizations, and oral legends presumably antedate them; none of the world's major cultures has been free of vampire fears. Jungians, Freudians and other enquirers into the nature of the human psyche have concluded that the vampire must therefore embody any number of our deepest anxieties, uncertainties and desires. More credulous souls have concluded that the ubiquity of vampire folklore is proof positive that these creatures exist. Let us examine the evidence.

AROUND THE WORLD IN EIGHTY VAMPIRES
Well, roughly

The Ancient World

Assyria. The oldest records of vampiric belief come from the Assyrians, who recognized many distinct classes of vampire, including the *ekimmu* and the *utukku*.

Babylon. The Sumerians of Babylon shared many of the Assyrian beliefs about *ekimmu*; they left us the earliest known depictions of vampires, on a cylinder seal. The Babylonian vampire-goddess Lilitu seems to have been taken over by the Hebrews as Lilith, who thus became the earliest-named vampire in the Judaeo-Christian tradition. Created to be a wife for Adam, she fled to the forces of darkness.

Ancient Greece. The *empusa*, a bloodsucking, flesh-eating demon which can take the form of a seductive woman; mentioned by Philostratus, who also writes of the *lamia*, made famous in the English-speaking world by Keats's poem. The original Lamia was the Queen of Libya, whose children were slaughtered by Hera, and who sought revenge by sucking infant blood. Her successors were called *lamiae*, or sometimes *larvae* or *lemures*. Classical Greece was also plagued by the *anthesteria*, the *ephialtae* and the *mormo*.

The Roman world. Took over its vampiric mythologies from Greece, and added some of its own, most famously the *strix* (plural *striges*), a night-owl given to sucking the blood of children.

Europe, East and West

Note that England, France, Portugal, Spain, Holland, Belgium, Wales and a few other European nations have little or no indigenous vampire mythology, nor any specialist terms for the undead themselves. However, most if not all of these countries do have some history of vampire attacks – especially England and France. (Much the same is true of the United States, even though it has been the world's largest recycler of European vampire mythology, thanks to the global triumph of American movies.)

Albania. As well as the Greek *vrykolakas*, Albania is home to the *sampiro*, a relative of the Slavic vampire, and the *kukuthi*, also known as the *lugat*.

Bosnia. The *lampir*, which usually manifests itself at times of (otherwise non-supernatural) plague.

Bulgaria. Home of the *ubour*, which has only one nostril and a sting at the end of its tongue; it also, for some reason, emits sparks at night (see below, 'How Do You Recognize a Vampire?'). The process by which an *ubour* forms is unusually disgusting: the corpse remains in its grave for forty days, swelled up with a gelatine-like muck until a new skeleton is formed. Bulgaria is also home to the *vampir* and the *krvoijac*. Also to the *ustrel*, which preys only on cattle, and is thought to be the returned form of a child who died on a Saturday without the benefit of baptism.

Croatia. The land teems with undead, in a number of subspecies: *tenjac, vukodlak, kosac, pijawica, prikosac . . .*

Denmark. The *mara*, a form of incubus or – more commonly – succubus.

Estonia. Three known vampire species: the *veripard* or 'blood-beard', the *vampiir* and the *vere-imeja* – 'bloodsucker'.

Germany. The *alp*, usually male, is a vampire-like spirit which usually targets women; similar to an incubus. The *dubbelsuger* or *doppelsauger*: literally, 'double-sucker', because a weaned child will become a vampire if it nurses again after death. Also the *nachzehrer*, which has the unusual habit, while lying in its coffin, of clutching one of its thumbs and keeping one of its eyes permanently open; it begins its vampiric career by consuming its own shroud, then parts of its own flesh . . . The *neuntöter*, or 'nine-killer', so called because it takes nine days for the vampire to form after a body is buried; it can be killed in slightly bathetic manner, by putting a lemon in its mouth. And, in Prussia, the *gierach*.

Greece. 'In no country has the Vampire tradition more strongly prevailed and more persistently maintained its hold upon the people than in modern Greece . . .' (Montague Summers, *The Vampire in Europe*). Novelists and film-makers have been slow to pick up on Greece as a vampiric *heimat*, one major exception being Simon Raven in his novel *Doctors Wear Scarlet*, which is about a young Cambridge classicist who travels to Minos and elsewhere in pursuit of ancient religions, and comes home strangely altered . . .

The classic form of Greek vampire is the *vrykolakas*. If the *vrykolokas* knocks at your door and calls out your name, you die the next day. But the country is also home to a very unusual type of vampire, the *callicantzaro*, which develops from a child born between Christmas Day and Epiphany (6 January), and then departs to live in the underworld, but comes back once a year to predate its own family and neighbours.

Hungary. Hungary's vampires include the more than familiar *vampir*, and the *liderc nadaly*, which has to be seen off with a nail in the temple.

> Hungary, it may not untruly be said, shares with Greece and Slovakia the reputation of being that particular region of the world which is most terribly infested by the Vampire and where he is seen at his ugliest and worst. Nor is this common reputation undeserved. It was owing to a number of extraordinary and terrible occurrences towards the end of the seventeenth century, which visitations persisted into the earlier years of the eighteenth century, that general attention was drawn to the problem of the Vampire . . .
> Montague Summers, *The Vampire in Europe* (1929).

Ireland. The *dearg-due or dearg-dul*, whose name signifies 'sucker of red blood'; and perhaps the female *leanhaum-shee*, not precisely a vampire but much given to vampiric ways.

Italy. Unlike the civilization dominated by ancient Rome, modern Italy has not been particularly rich in indigenous vampire myths, though the folkloric witch or *strega* sometimes saps the vitality of children in vampiric mode.

Montenegro. The *tenatz* – usually created when a cat jumps over a corpse.

Poland. The principal forms are the *upior* (alternatively *upier*, male form, and *upierzyca*, female form), noted for its thirst, extreme even by vampiric standards. (When staked, it gushes forth enormous quantities of blood.) Unlike many other European vampires, the *upior* possesses a forked tongue. Poland is also home to the *ohyn*, whose telltale sign is that it is born with a caul and a fully mature set of teeth; and to the *vjiesce*.

Portugal. The *bruxsa*, a female vampire who flies around at night in the shape of a giant bird. Unlike almost every other vampire species, she is utterly indestructible. But the Portuguese otherwise have little to worry about on the undead front, as vampires are rare in their country.

Romania. The general term for vampires is *strigoii*, or 'dead vampire'; the other Romanian term *moroii* specifies a particular subspecies of 'living vampire'. In the Wallachia region – Dracula's homeland – the local vampire is called *muroni* or *murony* or *muronul*, notorious in those parts for being able to shape-shift (like Dracula himself) into a variety of animal forms: dogs, cats, spiders, even fleas. Unlike the Count, the *muroni* attack leaves no telltale puncture wounds . . . but is no less lethal for that. Folklorists have also identified other Romanian vampire species: the *zmeu* (which can manifest itself in the shape of a flame), the *priculics*, the *varcolaci* and – of course – the *nosferatu*.

Russia. A land embarrassed with vampiric riches. The basic form is the *upir* or *upyr*, the ranks of which fiend were across the centuries swelled with newcomers: the *viesczy*, the *veripard*, the *upior* and *wampir*, the *upar* and the *upur*, and the *vourdalak*, one of the 'beautiful women' vampires. The *Alp*, usually male, is a vampire-like spirit which usually targets women; similar to an incubus. There was also the *eretica* (plural: *ereticy*), formed from the clay of a woman who had sold her soul to the devil; variants of this name include *eretik* and *erestun*.

Scotland. The *baobhan-sith*, a bloodsucking demon that could adopt the shape of a lovely woman, and so lure naive men to their deaths.

Serbia. The *vampir* and the *vukodlak* – the latter term originally meaning 'werewolf'.

Slovenia. The *kudlak*, a local vampire – every self-respecting village had one – which was kept in check by the attentions of the vampire slayers: *kresnik* or *krsnik*. Also the *nelapsi*, which can kill with a single glance, and will wipe out all life in a district, cattle, pets and humans alike. And the *pijavica*, found near the Italian and Austrian borders.

Wales. Though Welsh vampires are not numerous, the Land of Song was also home to perhaps the strangest instance of all its kind: a vampire chair, which, according to folklore, bit anyone who sat in it and drank their blood.

Africa and the Middle East

Africa. The *Adze*, a vampire spirit which travels in the form of a firefly, but reverts to humanoid shape if trapped; native to south-western Ghana and southern Togo. Also the *asanbosam* (or *asanbonsam*), known to the Ashanti of southern Ghana and along the Ivory Coast; and the *obayifo*, again known to the Ashanti. It can destroy crops as well as people.

The Middle East. The *algul*, a vampiric demon which according to region and literature takes many forms; it appears in the *Arabian Nights*, and provides English with the word 'ghoul'. (Ghouls, who frequent churchyards, are often female.) It has a near relative, the *aluga* or *aluka*, a bloodsucking demon mentioned in Proverbs (30.15). Also the *estrie*, an evil spirit that stalked the Hebrews, flying about by night and preying particularly on children.

Asia and Australasia

Australasia. The *mrart*, among some aboriginal peoples, would try to drag its victims away from the safety of the nocturnal campfire. Also the *Talamaur*, a kind of living vampire in the Banks Islands.

China. The *kuang-shi*, (alternatively *chiang-shi*), which is covered with green or white fur (possibly inspired by the mould that grows on a corpse in damp climates?), and has blazing red eyes. Like Dracula, it can turn itself into a mist; it can fly too, and become invisible. Also the *chang kuei*, the *hsi-hsue-kuei* ('suck-blood-demon'), and the *p'o*.

Burma. A vampire deity called *swawmx*. Also the *karens* and the *kephn* – the latter taking the form of a wizard's head and entrails, floating in mid-air.

India. The *buhta* (also *bhut*), a vampire created, usually, by violent death or suicide, or inappropriate funeral rites; they haunt cemeteries, but also all dark, remote places. They are sometimes worshipped as a semi-deity. Also the *brahmaparush*, a particularly unsavoury character, who drinks blood from his victim's skull and then performs a victory dance, with the deceased's entrails wrapped around his head like a turban; the *chordewa* of Bengal, which takes the shape of a black vampire cat; the horrific female *churel* or *churail*, created when a pregnant woman dies, especially at the festival of Diwali; the *gayal* or *ut*, a vampiric ghost, evolved from the spirit of a man who dies without a male heir or unmarried, so that there is no one to see to proper funeral rites. But there are many, many others: the *hant-pare*, the *hantu-dor dong*, the *hanh saburo*, the *masan*, the *pacu-pati* (meaning 'master of the herd', since he is the lord of all evil things), the *penanggalan*, the *pisacha* (revenant forms of the criminal and the insane), the *rakshasa* and the *vetala* (which rides astride a green horse, and may not always be wicked).

Japan. The hideous *hannya*, usually female in form, is the subject of many paintings. Also the *Kasha*, ghouls who feed hungrily on corpses.

Java. The *sundal bolong* is the revenant form of a woman who has been raped, impregnated and driven to suicide. She appears in white, and drains young men of all their blood.

Malaysia. The *bajang*, which takes the form of a ferocious polecat, but can be tamed and taught to be a loyal household servant, especially by wizards. The *langsuir*, a flying vampire which can transform itself into a woman of stunning beauty; created when a woman dies in childbirth, or from the shock of hearing that her child is stillborn. The unfortunate stillborn infant itself becomes another type of vampire, the *pontianak* or *mati-anak*. The *pelesit*, a kind of miniature vampire spirit, sneaks into the body of its victim, causing delirium (the unfortunate will start raving about cats) and ultimately death. The *penanggalan*, somewhat like the Burmese *kephn*, takes the shape of a flying creature made up solely of head, neck and dangling entrails – which glow in the dark. Always female, it takes particular delight in sucking the blood of women in labour.

Philippines. The *aswang*, a beautiful woman by day, a flying predator by night. It lands on rooftops and inserts its long, thin tongue in through the tiniest gaps, sucking blood from those sleeping below, especially children. Also the *danag*, which used to live and work in harmony with mankind until one fatal day when a woman accidentally cut her finger; the *Danang* sucked, and then sucked some more . . . And the *mandurugo* ('bloodsucker'), yet another instance of the beautiful-woman-by-day-flying-terror-by-night model.

Tibet. This Buddhist country's rich theology incorporates all manner of fiends, many of whom are vampiric. The most terrifying of these vampires is the *ahayankara*, a creature so mind-shatteringly evil that he is referred to, simply, as the Awful One.

The Americas

Brazil. The *jaracacas*, a snake-like creature, is not strictly a vampire but does feed vampire-like on the breasts on nursing mothers. Then there is the *lobishomen*, which seldom kills its female victims but leaves them prone (or supine) to nymphomania. (The word is almost certainly derived from an older Portuguese term meaning 'werewolf'.)

The Caribbean. In the West Indies you could encounter the *loogaroo*, which ought to be a werewolf (as the term is a corruption of the French word *loup-garou*, which underwent mutation as it travelled to the Caribbean by way of Guinea and the Congo), but is actually a vampiric old woman who receives power from Satan provided she repeatedly offers him blood sacrifices. She gains this blood by climbing up a special tree, peeling off her skin, and flying through the night in search of inhabited houses. (You can fend her off by putting grains of rice or sand in front of your house, since the *loogaroo* is an obsessive-compulsive creature which has to pick up every grain individually before she can carry out her vile intent – and seldom completes the fiddly task before dawn, when her evil powers wane.)

Mexico. The *civatateo* of the Aztecs, reported back to Europe in the sixteenth century; white-faced and hideous, they were originally noblewomen who had died in childbirth. Rather like traditional European witches, they rode on broomsticks and congregated to hold sabbats, especially at crossroads after dark.

THE VAMPIRE EPIDEMICS

The vampire is both eternal and ubiquitous. So why did the creature suddenly seize the imagination of Europe's thinkers and poets in the eighteenth century? Why were vampires so much on the mind in the Enlightenment and the Romantic periods? Answer: the so-called 'Vampire Epidemics', a series of crises that were reported from the late seventeenth century onwards, and fascinated both the credulous and the hard-headed. As a sardonic French writer (Collin de Plancy) put it in the 1820s:

> The most astonishing thing about these accounts of vampirism is that they shared the honour of astounding the eighteenth century with our greatest philosophers. They terrified Prussia, Silesia, Bohemia and the whole of Northern Europe, at precisely the same time as wise men in England and France were attacking superstition and popular error with the utmost confidence.

The epidemics had taken place in:
✝ Istria (1672).
✝ East Prussia (1710 and again in 1721).
✝ Hungary (1725–30).
✝ Austrian Serbia (1725–32; see the case of Arnold Paole, opposite).

✝ East Prussia (1750).

✝ Silesia (1755).

✝ Wallachia (1756).

✝ Russia (1772).

Most of the pioneering works of scholarship and imagination on vampires were published while these events were still either current or fresh in the memory. Cardinal Giuseppe Davanzati published his *Dissertations on Vampires* in 1744; Calmet's famous book appeared in 1746. The first modern poem on vampires, August Ossenfelder's *'Der Vampir'*, was written just two years later, in 1748, and was followed by several more German poems, though Goethe's vampire poem 'The Bride of Corinth' was not composed until almost the end of the century, in 1797.

In some cases, the outbreaks caused such popular distress that they were made the subject of official enquiries. One report in particular caught the imagination of all Europe.

✝HE CASE OF ARNOLD PAOLE (AKA PAUL)

Probably the single best-documented vampire story ever, this took place in Serbia from 1731 to 1732. Paole, a former soldier, returned to his native village of Meduegna, near Belgrade, after a tour of duty in Greece and the Levant. Once again, that region is at the root of the evil: Paole reported having been attacked by a vampire when he was stationed near Gossowa, in Turkish Serbia; he managed to destroy the creature, but felt as if he had been left under a curse.

Not long after his return, Paole suffered a fall from a hay wagon and died. But, a month later, villagers claimed to have seen Paole wandering around. Four people were said to have been killed, and cattle attacked. A group of soldier-medics was dispatched from Belgrade to investigate. They opened Paole's grave, and found that his body was not even slightly decomposed, that new nails had grown from his fingers and toes, that his jaw was gaping open and had blood trickling from it. They drove a stake through his heart; he screamed, and a large amount of blood gushed out. The body was burned and the ashes reburied . . . The official report, *Visum et Repertum* – picked up by the press, and spread across the continent – was so detailed and dispassionate that it persuaded many a former sceptic that vampires were indeed real.

What was going on here? Among the range of rational explanations, the most likely is premature burial – not such an uncommon mistake in an age which had not yet thoroughly studied the symptoms which indicate full death rather than catalepsy or trance states. Whatever was going on in Serbia, Paole's story struck the imagination of Europe so resoundingly that, within a matter of months, even the urbane poet Alexander Pope was making jokes about having become a vampire.

Of Camp and Vamp: a Note on Montague Summers

The undoubted master in the field of vampire folklore is Alphonsus Joseph-Mary Augustus Montague Summers (1880–1948). And for the last seven or eight decades, almost everyone who has written on the folklore of vampirism has been indebted to his two works of quite prodigious scholarship: *The Vampire: His Kith and Kin* (1928) and *The Vampire in Europe* (1929). Summers was an ordained Anglican deacon (probably), Roman Catholic priest (self-appointed, probably), Uranian poet, schoolteacher, occultist, outstanding scholar and editor of the Restoration drama and the Gothic novel, alleged pederast (acquitted), eccentric, flamboyant homosexual and all-round larger-than-life man of letters.

Though sometimes spiteful on the page, by all accounts he was delightful, if strange, company, and he maintained vehemently that all of the occult phenomena he researched were entirely real, including vampires. There are rumours to the effect that he may have dabbled in the dark arts at some point in his youth. It's possible that the intemperate nature of his condemnations and comminations – at exactly the time when scholars were starting to rehabilitate witches as cruelly persecuted scapegoats, Summers stoutly maintained that at least some of the witches persecuted in Europe and America were authentic tools of Satan – owes something to his wish or need to set his immature follies at a distance. Oddly, his fervent anti-Satanic stance did not prevent him from making friends with Aleister Crowley, the 'Wickedest Man in the World'.

In person, Summers was an impressive sight: huge, lumbering and dressed in clothes that were reminiscent of an eighteenth-century clergyman (though friends and foes alike said that his true spiritual homeland was the Middle Ages). He affected a very odd hairstyle, swept back from the brow into two earmuff-like curlicues – a little like Princess Leia in the *Star Wars* films. He could be seen waddling out of the British Museum Reading Room, as one eyewitness described him, in 'black soutane and cloak, with buckled shoes – à la Louis Quatorze – and shovel hat . . .' Under his arm he would carry a large portfolio, with the word VAMPIRES written across it in blood-red capitals. He also affected an ornate cane, its silver handle depicting Leda being raped by Zeus in the form of a swan. He is probably the twentieth century's best candidate for a Van Helsing figure, and would make a meaty subject for a biopic.

WHAT DOES 'VAMPIRE' MEAN?

Here is Dom Augustin Calmet's account, from 1746:

> The Apparitions (Revenans) of Hungary, or Vampires . . . are men who have been dead for some considerable time, it may be for a long period or it may be for a shorter period, and these

issue forth from their graves and come to disturb the living, whose blood they suck and drain. These vampires visibly appear to men, they knock loudly at their doors and cause the sound to re-echo throughout the whole house, and once they have gained a foothold death generally follows. To this sort of Apparition is given the name Vampire or Oupire, which in the Slavonic tongue means a bloodsucker. The only way to obtain deliverance from their molestations is by disinterring the dead body, by cutting off the head, by driving a stake through the breast, by transfixing the heart, or by burning the corpse to ashes.

Montague Summers, in *The Vampire: His Kith and Kin*, goes a little deeper into the realms of etymology:

> The word Vampire (also vampyre) is from the Magyar *vampir*, a world of Slavonic origin occurring in the same form in Russian, Polish, Czech, Serbian and Bulgarian with such variants as Bulgarian, *vapir*, *vepir*; Ruthenian *vepyr*, *vopyr*, *opyr*; Russian *upir*, *upyr*; South Russian *upuir*; Polish *upier* . . .

Although Summers never quite settles upon a true source, he entertains the possibility, accepted by some other scholars, that the root of the word is an Indo-European verb meaning 'to drink'.

HOW DO YOU BECOME A VAMPIRE?

Everyone who has seen a Hollywood vampire film knows this: you turn into a vampire after being fatally bitten by one; or, in some versions of the mythology, by drinking the vampire's own blood. But folklore provides many other ways of becoming undead.

One of these is by practising Black Magic. Bram Stoker, through the mouthpiece of Van Helsing, hints that this may have been the way

Dracula was turned. 'He dared even to attend the Scholomance . . .' (Chapter XXIII). The 'Scholomance', otherwise known as the 'school of solomonari', was something Stoker found mentioned in Emily Gerard's writings on the superstitions of Transylvania. The solomonari were wizards, or shamans, who could control the weather (an ability the Count is said to possess) and ride dragons through the sky. Solomonari were born with cauls and tails; they grew up to be huge, with red eyes and red hair. Some time around puberty, the budding solomonari are kidnapped and taken to the Scholomance, where they undergo iniatory ordeals for as long as twenty years, and learn various magic arts, including the ability to shape-shift. Remarkably few of the imaginative works inspired by *Dracula* have picked up this hint.

Other ways include:

✝ By committing suicide.

✝ By dying without the benefit of baptism.

✝ By having a cat or some other animal walk over your corpse. (This odd belief crops up in many cultures, from Romania to China.)

✝ By being born on Christmas Day (and so, presumably, blasphemously upstaging God on Christ's birthday), or between Christmas Day and Epiphany.

✝ By committing a crime and getting away with it in your lifetime (in Albania).

✝ By being born to a mother who uses a horse's collar to ease the pain of labour (in Germany).

✝ By having blue eyes (in the Balkans).

✝ By being a corpse exposed to strong moonlight, and thus flooded with powerful yang forces (in China).

✝ By drowning (in Croatia and elsewhere).

✝ By being a seventh son (in Romania and elsewhere); or worse, the seventh son of a seventh son.

HOW DO YOU RECOGNIZE A VAMPIRE?

A Vampire is generally described as being exceedingly gaunt and lean with a hideous countenance and eyes wherein are glinting the red fire of perdition. When, however, he has satiated his lust for warm human blood his body becomes horribly puffed and bloated, as though he were some great leech gorged and replete to bursting. Cold as ice, or it may be fevered and burning as a hot coal, the skin is deathly pale, but the lips are very full and rich, blub [*sic*] and red; the teeth white and gleaming, and the canine teeth wherewith he bites deep into the neck of his prey to suck thence the vital streams which re-animate his body and invigorate all his forces appear notably sharp and pointed. Often his mouth curls back in a vulpine snarl which bares these fangs, 'a gaping mouth and gleaming teeth', says Leone Allacci, and so in many districts the hare-lipped are avoided as being certainly vampires. In Bulgaria, it is thought that the Vampire who returns from the tomb has only one nostril; and in certain districts of Poland he is supposed to have a sharp point at the end of his tongue, like the sting of a bee. It is said that the palms of a Vampire's hands are downy with hair, and the nails are always curved and crooked, often well-nigh the length of a great bird's claw, the quicks dirty and foul with clots and gouts of black blood. His breath is unbearably fetid and rank with corruption, the stench of the charnel . . .

Montague Summers, *The Vampire: His Kith and Kin* (1928)

TWO REAL-LIFE 'VAMPIRES'

Vampire fiction has long been haunted by two historical 'vampires', neither of them supernatural, but both of them bloodthirsty enough to win Dracula's grudging respect.

Gilles de Rais, aka 'Bluebeard' (1404–40). Though he earned the right to be regarded as a French national hero for his exploits in the Hundred Years' War – he fought side-by-side with Joan of Arc against the English – he is mainly remembered for his later civilian activities and hobbies. Immensely wealthy, and sometimes called 'the richest Baron in France', he spent much of his fortune on pursuing the dark arts, a practice which included murdering many of his neighbours, especially young boys. Arrested and tortured, he eventually confessed to horrifying acts of sadism, violence . . . and vampirism. He was duly executed. Some of his modern notoriety is due to the detailed evocation of his atrocities in J.-K. Huysmans's novel of satanism, *Là-Bas* (1891), whose protagonist, Durtal, is writing a history of the bloody baron.

Elizabeth (Erzsebet) Bathory, aka 'Countess Dracula' (1560–1614). Apart from Vlad the Impaler, the most influential of all historical figures on vampire mythology is the Hungarian noblewoman commonly referred to either as 'the Bloody Countess' or – evocatively if inaccurately – 'Countess Dracula'. She lived from 1560–1614; thus, to put these dates into perspective, she enjoyed a lifetime that overlapped fairly closely with that of William Shakespeare. According to legend, the countess developed her sanguinary ways when her husband was away fighting the Turk and she was left with time on her hands in Castle Čachtice, not too far from Bratislava. Obsessed with maintaining her youthful good looks, and drawn to occult practices, she decided that her ideal moisturizer was the blood of serving girls. Accordingly, she drew pints and pints of the fluid from her household staff, and bathed in it.

Estimates of the number of maidens she actually slaughtered for her beauty regime start at around fifty and go all the way up to six hundred and more. She was eventually arrested for her crimes in

1610, and punished by being walled up in her own bedroom, provided with food through a narrow slot. Of the many, many films that have been inspired by her atrocities, the most famous are Harry Kumel's *Daughters of Darkness* (1971), which stars Delphine Seyrig as a full-blown vampiric version of Elizabeth, still alive and chic in the twentieth century, and *Countess Dracula* (1971), with Ingrid Pitt in the title role. Stoker knew of the story from Sabine Baring-Gould's *The Book of Werewolves* (1865), which contained the first lengthy account of her exploits in English.

'PSYCHIC VAMPIRES'

Towards the end of the Victorian age, doctors began to speculate about – or, in some cases, affirm the existence of – the so-called 'psychic' vampire: a human who did not literally suck blood, but who somehow manage to leech all the vitality from those around them. This became a popular theme of spooky fiction: see, for example, Algernon Blackwood's story 'The Transfer'; Sir Arthur Conan Doyle's 'The Parasite'; and Reginald Hodder's novel *The Vampire*. In 1896, a physician – Dr Franz Hartmann – wrote a report of just such a case that had come to his attention. Such creatures, he says,

> unconsciously vampirize every sensitive person with whom they come into contact, and they instinctively seek out such persons and invite them to stay at their houses. I know of an old lady, a vampire, who thus ruined the health of a lot of robust servant girls, whom she took into her service and made them sleep in her room. They were all in good health when they entered, but soon they began to sicken, they became emaciated and consumptive and had to leave the service.

WHY BATS?

Bats are now a universally recognized symbol of all things vampiric, and everyone knows that Count Dracula can turn himself into a bat. In fact, though Stoker has a few telling bat references in his novel, the latter idea only became fixed in the popular imagination after 1927, when the stage version of *Dracula* stunned and thrilled audiences with a very simple trick involving a large cloak and a wooden flittermouse. (The notion that vampires wear long cloaks, preferably with a high raised collar above the back of the head, also dates from this production; the cloak was designed to facilitate a disappearing trick involving a trapdoor. If the actor playing the Count stood with his back to the audience and spread his 'wings', his head and body could not be seen, and he could drop below stage, leaving an empty cloak to crumble.) Tod Browning's film of 1931 carried these motifs over, and the rest is vampire history (see Chapter Four).

Before the 1920s, the bat link was much more tentative. It had only crept into folklore during the sixteenth century, when explorers in South America sent home reports of a bat that lived by sucking (actually by lapping) blood from horses, cattle and human beings. Apart from this fluke of zoology, the only grounds for associating bats with vampires is their habit of sleeping by day and hunting by night – that and, according to some legends, the fact that they are the only two types of mammals capable of self-powered flight. The association is something of a species libel, as bats are delightful to watch and useful in keeping down numbers of flies and other annoying insects. The Chinese have traditionally regarded bats as symbols of good fortune.

Darwin and the Vampire Bat

Until well into the nineteenth century, it was widely suspected that reports of the vampire bat in South America were merely tall tales, and that the creature was a legend. But Charles Darwin himself, in *A Naturalist's Voyage Around the World*, was able to prove that the creature was real:

> We were bivouacking late one night near Coquimbo in Chile, when my servant, noticing that one of the horses was very restive went to see what was the matter, and fancying he could detect something, suddenly put his hand on the beast's withers, and secured the vampire.

JUNG AND EASILY FREUDENED

Sigmund Freud, who was formulating the earliest version of psychoanalysis in the same years when Stoker was preparing *Dracula*, had surprisingly little to say on the subject of vampires, even in his much-cited essay on 'The Uncanny'. No matter: his disciples and groupies have more than made up for this silence, particularly since the 1960s. The Freudians usually begin with the classic vampire attack: a man enters the bed chamber of a young, usually comely woman; he penetrates her body; fluids are exchanged. Aha! There is something sexual about this! Gosh, do you think so?

Then, since livings have to be earned, it all becomes a bit more complicated. The Freudian yarn about the Oedipus complex is reeled out, so that Dracula become the Big Daddy, and his attacks are therefore read as (a) re-enactions of the Primal Scene, in which the child discovers the parents *in flagrante*, and/or (b) at least in symbolic terms, incestuous. (If you're a politicized Freudian, you see the whole novel as an allegory of patriarchal power, threatened by unleashed female eroticism but restored by a posse of father figures. Discuss.) Biting (i.e. oral sadism) refers us back to infantile aggression during breastfeeding; vamps are dead, so the necrophilia card can be played. Most vampire fables include some guy-on-guy or girl-on-girl action, so that allows homoeroticism into the party. It's not a hard game to play, once you get the hang of it.

Carl Jung, the favoured son who rebelled against the Freudian system in the appropriate Oedipal manner and built an analytic house of his own, played down the erotic side of the vampire myth and assimilated it to his more general ideas about the 'shadow' – roughly, the dark side of our personalities that we disown, ignore or struggle with, but which has to find some form of expression. Vampire legends and fictions are, according to this line, a particular embodiment of the selfish, violently antisocial impulses on which we would all act were we not tightly wrapped by civilization.

By the way, Freud appears as a character in a little-known play, *Vampire*, by the English dramatist Snoo Wilson. And the American writer Camille Paglia has suggested that the most influential of Freud's followers, Jacques Lacan, was himself a vampire. (This may have been either a throwaway insult or a moral protest; it is hard to tell.) Her book *Sexual Personae* teems with vampire lore, so she ought to know.

Succubi and Incubi

Though not precisely vampires, these creatures from medieval demonology had – or have – a great deal in common with the undead. But where a vampire stalks the night in search of food, the succubus (female) or incubus (male) has a quite different goal in mind: sex. Intercourse with a demon was often held to be the explanation for erotic dreams. In recent years, it has also been suggested that the sense of helpless paralysis often reported by victims might be attributed to the actual state of mild paralysis that is a normal part of the nightly sleep cycle. Probably the most famous depiction of an incubus occurs in Fuseli's fantastical painting *The Nightmare*, in which the night visitor crouched on a swooning woman is a small, nasty, goblin-like being – not at all a romantic seducer.

How Do You Get Rid of a Vampire?

The methods that have become standard since Stoker – the crucifix, the holy wafer and holy water, the Bible – were seldom if ever called on when dealing with folkloric vampires. Curiously enough, almost every culture from Romania to China agrees that garlic is a highly effective deterrent, though no one has ever conclusively established why this should be the case; faith in its powers appears to go all the way back to ancient Egypt. In China and Malaysia, parents used to wipe garlic on the heads of their children to ward off attack; in the Philippines, it was applied under the armpit, like a deodorant. In parts of central Europe, corpses were sometimes buried with garlic stuffed into their mouths and nostrils, and rubbed over the eyelids, to prevent future nastiness. Hollywood has remembered these practices, and sometimes made fun of them, but it has largely been forgotten that hawthorn also has powerful anti-vampiric properties. (Two of the very few films to reinstate this belief are *The Satanic Rites of Dracula* and the television film *Salem's Lot*.)

When it comes to the crunch, vampires must – of course – be staked, and preferably decapitated, then burned. The whole business about being allergic to sunlight is, alas, of no great vintage, and only appeared in 1922 with Murnau's *Nosferatu* – Stoker's Count is perfectly able to walk around in sunlight, though his occult powers are gravely reduced. Bullets are reported to be effective on some Romanian vampires, but the whole business about silver bullets, or silver in general, has little if any warrant in folklore, and has entered the tradition mainly thanks to the efforts of screenwriters. The oddest folkloric method for vampire disposal involves stealing his left sock, filling it with stones or other weights, and throwing it outside the town or village limits; though any vampire sluggish enough to let you steal his sock can hardly be all that threatening.

†WO

ROMANTIC AND VICTORIAN VAMPIRES, 1816–97

In which the ancient fiend leaps from legend to literature

†HE BYRONIC VAMPIRE

In the beginning, there was the Lord.

Lord Byron, that is, for the story of modern vampirism is generally agreed to begin with George Gordon, Lord Byron (1788–1824); his new friend Percy Shelley and Percy's wife-to-be Mary Godwin; Byron's pregnant eighteen-year-old mistress, Jane 'Claire' Clairmont; and his personal doctor, the twenty-year-old John William Polidori. The place was the Villa Diodati, on the shore of Lake Geneva; and the date 18 June 1816. There have been many, many accounts of this summer house party and its consequences; two of the most famous are by those who participated. Here is Mary Shelley, looking back on those days from 1831:

> . . . it proved a wet, uncongenial summer, and incessant rain often confined us for days to the house. Some volumes of ghost stories translated from the German into French, fell into our hands . . .

(Scholars have established that this collection must have been a volume entitled *Fantasmagoriana, ou recueil d'histoires d'apparitions, de spectres, revenants, etc*, translated by Jean-Baptiste Benoît Eyriès, 1812. Snappy title.)

'We will each write a ghost story', said Lord Byron, and his proposition was acceded to. There were four of us. [*Sic:* Claire Clairmont was evidently left out of the literary game.] The noble author began a tale, a fragment of which he printed at the end of his poem of Mazeppa. Shelley, more apt to embody ideas and sentiments in the radiance of brilliant imagery, and in the music of the most melodious verse that adorns our language, than to invent the machinery of a story, commenced one founded on the experiences of his early life. Poor Polidori had some terrible idea about a skull-headed lady, who was punished for peeping through a keyhole – what to see I forget – something very shocking and wrong of course . . . The illustrious poets also, annoyed by the platitude of prose, speedily relinquished their uncongenial task.

But Mary herself, she explained, was tormented by a failure of imagination. For day after day, she strained to come up with a tale that might 'awaken thrilling horror'. Eventually, the subject she had been hunting for came to her in a kind of waking dream; it was, of course, the germ of her novel *Frankenstein*. Her account (taken from the introduction to the 1831 edition) is not, however, altogether reliable. The only surviving contemporary account is Polidori's diary entry for 18 June:

Began my ghost-story after tea. Twelve o'clock, really began to talk ghostly. L. B. [Byron] repeated some verses of Coleridge's *Christabel*, of the witch's breast; when silence ensued, and Shelley, suddenly shrieking and putting his hands to his head, ran out of the room with a candle. Threw water in his face, and afterwards gave him ether. He was looking at Mrs S., and suddenly thought of a woman he had heard of who had eyes instead of nipples, which, taking hold of his mind, horrified him . . .

THE POLIDORIAN VAMPYRE

Byron's fragment, which he brushed up a little for later publication, was left lying around the house and read by Polidori. He adapted it freely and called it 'The Vampyre'. It is the first fiction of its kind in the English language, the prototype for Bram Stoker's Count some eight decades later, and thus the original begetter of every vampire novel, play, film, opera, video game, ballet and soap opera that has flourished ever since. In Byron's draft, a poetic young aristocrat, Darvell, goes on a voyage to Turkey, where he dies in a graveyard – having vowed to return from the dead a month later.

During 'two or three idle mornings', Polidori bulked the yarn up to some twenty pages and made some radical changes. For one, Byron's virtuous hero Darvell became the villainous Lord Ruthven. The choice of name was barbed: a recently published novel by Byron's embittered ex-mistress Lady Caroline Lamb (it appeared on 9 May 1816, very shortly after Byron had left England for Geneva), *Glenarvon*, has as its central figure a barely veiled portrait of the poet as 'Clarence de Ruthven, Lord Glenarvon'.

In Polidori's version, Ruthven returns from Turkey and arrives in London in time for the Season. The story ends with the marriage of Ruthven and the narrator's sister.

. . . when they arrived, it was too late. Lord Ruthven had disappeared, and Aubrey's sister had glutted the thirst of a VAMPYRE!

Who Was Polidori?

Born 7 September 1795, he attended the Catholic school Ampleforth (1804–10), and then Edinburgh University, where he wrote a verse tragedy, eventually published as *Ximenes*. He qualified as a Doctor of Medicine early in 1815, when he was still only nineteen. Byron hired him as his private physician in 1816; unknown to Byron, the publisher John Murray had commissioned Polidori to keep a diary of the lord's exploits. After many quarrels, Byron finally fired Polidori in September 1816. He made his way to Milan, but was soon in trouble for insulting an officer, and was ordered to leave.

Back in England, Polidori tried to set himself up in his profession; he opened a dispensary, and joined a Masonic Lodge. In September, he suffered a concussion in a road accident. Still ambitious for literary glory, he published his *Essay Upon the Source of Positive Pleasure* in 1818; and, in 1819 – the year in which 'The Vampyre' was pirated – *Ximenes, The Wreath and Other Poems* and his one novel, *Ernestus Berchtold; or, The Modern Oedipus*. None of these productions brought him wealth or fame, so he resolved to qualify as a lawyer, and was admitted to Lincoln's Inn in 1820. This attempt was short-lived, as was Polidori himself; after publishing two more minor works, he died in August 1821, possibly by his own hand, though the official verdict was that the death was from natural causes.

Description of Lord Ruthven from 'The Vampyre'

> He gazed upon the mirth around him, as if he could not
> participate therein. Apparently, the light laughter of the fair only
> attracted his attention, that he might by a look quell it, and
> throw fear into those breasts where thoughtlessness reigned.
> Those who felt this sensation of awe, could not explain whence it
> arose: some attributed it to the dead grey eye . . .

In spite of the deadly hue of his face, which never gained a warmer tint, either from the blush of modesty, or from the strong emotion of passion, though its form and outline were beautiful, many of the female hunters after notoriety attempted to win his attentions . . .

VAMPIRES IN THE VOCABULARY

The word 'vampire' entered the English language in printed form in May 1732, in an article in the *Gentleman's Magazine* entitled 'Political Vampyres'. As the title suggests, it made its debut as a political symbol, rather than a mythological figure:

This account of *Vampyres*, you'll observe, comes from the Eastern Part of the World, always remarkable for its *Allegorical Style*. The States of Hungary are in subjection to the *Turks* and *Germans*, and govern'd by a pretty harsh Hand; which obliges them to couch all their complaints under *Figures* [i.e. metaphors] . . .

This is remarkably shrewd, not least in its recognition of the ways in which oppressed peoples may express their resistance through political allegories – an obvious enough idea for us today, since it was such a standard ploy of, say, artists in Eastern Europe during the period of Soviet rule, but far from a cliché in 1732. Incidentally, a variety of Russian authors in the nineteenth century – Gogol, Turgenev and Alexis Tolstoy (a distant cousin of Count Leo) – often used folkloric tales of vampires as a way of escaping tsarist censorship. The vampires in their tales are avaricious landlords, or brutal Cossacks.

This passage also anticipates countless thousands of modern critical essays by grasping the key fact that, whatever else vampires may be, they have an incorrigible tendency to act as metaphors.

Our author continues:

> History, especially our own, supplies us with so many Instances
> of Vampyres, in this sense, that it would fill Volumes to
> enumerate them . . .

> Some persons may be *Vampyres*, or *Blood-Suckers*, i.e. *Sharpers*,
> *Usurers*, and *Stockjobbers*, *unjust Stewards* and *the dry nurses of the*
> *Great Estates*; but nothing less than the Power of a *Treasury* can
> raise up a compleat *Vampyre*.

The earliest known reference to true vampires came just two years
later, in a book entitled *Travels of Three English Gentlemen* (first published
in 1734; reprinted in the *Harleian Miscellany*, Volume IV, 1745):

> These *Vampyres* are supposed to be the bodies of deceased
> persons, animated by evil spirits, which come out of the grave, in
> the night-time, suck the blood of many of the living, and thereby
> destroy them . . .

VAMPIRES IN THE LIBRARY

The first full-scale scholarly book on the subject was Dom Augustin
Calmet's work, known in English as *Treatise on the Vampires of Hungary
and Surrounding Regions*, first published in 1746 and widely read for
decades to come. Voltaire read it, and scorned it in his *Dictionnaire
philosophique*, but unfairly – Calmet was not nearly so credulous as
Voltaire made out. (Incidentally, Calmet's book is referred to in the
anonymous 'Introduction' to the first printing of Polidori's tale.)

THE ROMANTICS AND THEIR VAMPIRES

Polidori and Byron did not exactly have to cudgel their imaginations to come up with the subject of the undead. Even before the *Gentleman's Magazine* article, vampires had long been a popular subject among the European thinking classes, especially in Paris and London. They were particularly fascinated by the so-called 'vampire epidemics' of the late seventeenth and early eighteenth centuries (see Chapter 1).

The theme of folkloric vampirism was fairly common among the German Romantic writers, and crops up in the earlier English Romantics, too. But none of the writers before Polidori strayed very far from their sources in folklore and mythology. Polidori made the archetypical vampire posh; and contemporary; and male; and glamorous. The game was afoot.

Some Romantic Vampire Poems

Robert Southey, *Thalaba the Destroyer* (1799–1801). Southey had called Byron and Shelley the 'Satanic School' of poets, in acknowledgement of their affinities with Milton's arch-rebel in *Paradise Lost*, Satan, yet he dabbled in darkness himself, introducing a vampiric episode in *Thalaba the Destroyer* (Book VIII). Based on his browsing in the *Arabian Nights*, this epic of good versus evil depicts its hero, sheltering from a rainstorm in some ancient tombs, confronting a vampire who proves to be his late wife Oneiza – or, rather, the corpse of his wife, animated by a demon.

> *But in her eyes there dwelt*
> *Brightness more terrible*
> *Than all the loathsomeness of death.*

A Van Helsing before his time, Thalaba (egged on by an Old Man) takes pitiless action:

> *. . . through the vampire corpse*
> *He thrust his lance; it fell,*
> *And howling with the wound,*
> *Its fiendish tenant fled.*

The poem was later adapted for the stage, and produced in 1823.

John Stagg, **'The Vampire'** (1810), from *The Minstrel of the North*. Stagg, not often remembered these days, has the distinction of writing the first English poem devoted exclusively and unequivocally to vampires. He based his plot on the reports of European vampire epidemics: Stagg's vampire is the recently dead Sigismund, who attacks his former friend Herman and Herman's wife, Gertrude.

> *Just from that moment Gertrude drew*
> *From 'neath her cloke the hidden light;*
> *When, dreadful! She beheld in view*
> *The shade of Sigismund! sad sight!*
>
> *Indignant roll'd his ireful eyes,*
> *That gleam'd with wild horrific stare;*
> *And fix'd a moment with surprise,*
> *Beheld aghast th'enlightening glare.*
>
> *His jaws cadaverous were besmear'd*
> *With clotted carnage o'er and o'er,*
> *And all his horrid whole appeared*
> *Distent, and filled with human gore!*

Herman dies that night; the next day, villagers drive stakes through the hearts of both Herman and Sigismund.

Lord Byron, 'The Giaour: A Fragment of a Turkish Tale' (1813). Pronounced, roughly, 'jower', and meaning an infidel, a non-Muslim, this poem was one of Byron's most widely read productions. It includes this curse, cast upon the hero by a Muslim:

> *But first on earth, as Vampire sent*
> *Thy corse shall from its tomb be rent;*
> *Then ghastly haunt thy native place,*
> *And suck the blood of all thy race;*
> *There from thy daughter, sister, wife,*
> *At midnight drain the stream of life;*
> *Yet loathe the banquet which perforce*
> *Must feed thy livid living corse.*
> *Thy victims, ere they yet expire,*
> *Shall know the demon for their sire;*
> *As cursing thee, thou cursing them,*
> *Thy flowers are withered on the stem . . .*
>
> *Yet with thine own best blood shall drip*
> *Thy gnashing tooth and haggard lip;*
> *Then stalking to thy sullen grave,*
> *Go – and with Gouls and Afrits rave;*
> *Till these in horror shrink away*
> *From spectre more accursed than they!*

One of the folkloric influences on the poem appears to be the Greek legend of the *vrykolakas*, a corpse animated by demons which returns to prey on its own kin.

Samuel Taylor Coleridge, *Christabel* (1797). The first draft was composed as early as 1797, and was widely circulated in manuscript form, but not published until 1816. This was the poem that made Shelley shriek at the Villa Diodati. The offending lines were these:

> *Her silken robe and inner vest,*
> *Dropt to her feet, and full in view,*
> *Behold! her bosom and half her side—*
> *Hideous, deformed and pale of hue,*
> *O shield her! shield sweet Christabel!*

This may not be very shocking to readers who have supped deep on more graphic horrors, perhaps; and it does not obviously display the trademarks of a vampire. In fact, though *Christabel* is frequently cited as the first major vampire poem in English, and is sometimes included in anthologies of vampire literature, it never once uses the word 'vampire'; and though the villain of the piece, Geraldine, is unquestionably a malign supernatural being (and hardly less questionably a lesbian – the first of a Sapphic Regiment of Vampires), she may not be undead. William Empson, the most brilliant of Coleridge's editors, calls Geraldine not a vampire but a 'witch'.

But Coleridge deserves his honoured place in vampiric history, anyway, for the undead elements in *The Rime of the Ancient Mariner*. Thanks to the heroic researches of John Livingston Lowes in *The Road to Xanadu* (1927) we can be fairly sure that Coleridge had read (a) Voltaire's article on vampires in the *Dictionnaire philosophique*, (b) Calmet's book (see above, 'Vampires in the Library'), and (c) a paper by John Ferriar, M. D., 'Of Popular Illusions, and particularly of Medical Demonology', which had seven pages on vampires and dead bodies that have been reanimated by demons.

To this strange quintet of verses, we should add at least two distinctly vampiric poems by Keats: *Lamia* (1819) and *La Belle Dame sans Merci* (1819) – grandmother of all the seductive and deadly she-vampires who start to teem through the European imagination a few decades later.

THE VAMPIRE CRAZE BEGINS

Polidori was not responsible for publishing his vampire story. It appeared on the market in pirate form in the *New Monthly Magazine,* April 1819, courtesy of Colburn, the publishers of Lady Caroline Lamb's *Glenarvon,* and under Byron's name. An anonymous introduction explained all about the nature of vampires. ('The superstition upon which this tale is founded is very general in the East . . .') It sold briskly, and Colburn reissued it in pamphlet form, in French and German as well as English. The tale did particularly well in France, where it was sometimes included in editions of Byron's works. Indeed, a publisher who omitted it in one edition was obliged by popular protest to reinstate it. The initials L. B. appeared on the title pages of some editions, and almost everyone was convinced that it must be a kind of autobiography. Goethe, no less a prince of letters, came to the perverse, baffling conclusion that this brief supernatural melodrama was the British poet's finest production. (Goethe himself wrote a ballad, 'The Bride of Corinth', which included a vampire-like female.) Peeved both by the mistaken attribution of the piece – and by his lack of payment – Polidori wrote a stiff letter which appeared in the *New Monthly* in May:

Mr Editor,

As the person referred to in the Letter from Geneva, prefixed to the Tale of the Vampyre, in your last Number, I beg leave to state, that your correspondent has been mistaken in attributing that tale, in its present form, to Lord Byron. The fact is, that though the groundwork is certainly Lord Byron's, its development is mine, produced at the request of a lady, who denied the possibility of any thing being drawn from the materials which Lord Byron had said he intended to have employed in the formation of his Ghost story.

I am, &c. JOHN W. POLIDORI.

This was not enough. Polidori continued to nag Colburn until he was given the rather insultingly low fee of £30. Byron was even more annoyed, especially as it became clear that it had taken a squib by one of his ex-employees to cement his notoriety across Europe, and he instructed his publisher, John Murray, to publish his 'Fragment of a Story' as an appendix to his poem *Mazeppa*.

But it was too late. For the next three decades, the vampire was a Byronic lord (and, for the more credulous, Lord Byron was a vampire). More often than not, he was called Lord Ruthven, as in Cyprien Bérard's *Lord Ruthven, ou Les vampires*, a two-volume novel published in Paris in February 1820, and with a cheeky dedication to Byron. Bérard's book took the form of a literary Grand Tour, with stopovers in Venice, Florence, Naples, Modena, the Tyrol, Poland, Moravia, Athens, Benares and Baghdad. At each destination, the lord sampled a new bride. Ruthven was variously described as a 'Don Juan vampirique' and as a 'Lovelace of the tombs' – '*ce Lovelace des tombeaux*'.

The book ended with an appeal to the audience: 'We could perhaps publish Lord Ruthven's *History of My First Life* if we are encouraged to do so by some success with this publication.'

ANCESTORS OF THE BYRONIC VAMPIRE

Byron has sometimes been called 'the first celebrity'. He was certainly one of the first authors ever to cultivate what we now call an 'image'; or, more exactly, partly to encourage, partly to acquiesce in the spread of legends about his delicious wickedness. It was whispered, for example, that Byron had murdered his mistress, and 'enjoyed drinking her blood, from a cup made of her cranium'. Both the author and his thrilled audience had a handful of wicked precedents or role models in mind, both fictional and real:

✝ Milton's Satan. (Byron and Shelley believed that Milton had stayed at the Villa Diodati. A nice legend, but quite wrong: Milton died long before the villa was built.)

✝ Lord Rochester.

✝ Lord George Selwyn. 'If Lord George Selwyn returns, let him in by all means. If I am still alive I shall be pleased to see him; if not, he will be pleased to see me' – Lord Holland on his deathbed; reported by Horace Walpole.

✝ Thomas Warton.

✝ Sir John Lambert.

✝ Hero/villains from the dramas of Thomas Otway.

✝ The gothic villains of Mrs Radcliffe.

Marks of the Byronic Vampire

It was one of those faces which, having once beheld, we never afterwards forget. It seemed as if the soul of passion had been stamped and printed upon every feature. The eye beamed into life as it threw up its dark ardent gaze, with a look nearly of inspiration, while the proud curl of the upper lip expressed haughtiness and bitter contempt; yet, even mixed with these fierce characteristics, an air of melancholy and dejection shaded over and softened every harsher expression.

On a portrait of Clarence de Ruthven,
in Lady Caroline Lamb's *Glenarvon* (1816)

The Byronic vampire is:

+ Aristocratic.
+ Handsome (or, at any rate, with powerful, compelling features).
+ Charismatic.
+ Haughty, disdainful, scowling.
+ Seductive.
+ Enigmatic, possibly hiding some dreadful crime or other secret.
+ Rebellious.
+ Melancholic.

And:

+ Doomed.

STAGE BLOOD: VAMPIRES IN THE THEATRE . . .

Virtually within days of *Lord Ruthven*'s publication, the figure of the vampire jumped like wildfire from Parisian page to Parisian stage. Jean Charles Emmanuel Nodier's *Le Vampire*, which was set in Scotland – *'une grotte basaltique'* in Staffa, to be exact – and featured 'Lord Rutwen' and 'Sir Aubray' as leading characters, premiered at the Théâtre de la Porte-Sainte-Martin while *Lord Ruthwen* was still a bestseller. Nodier's play launched an immediate craze. In the words of the vampire hunter Montague Summers (from *The Vampire: His Kith and Kin*; see Chapter Two):

> Immediately upon the furore created by Nodier's *Le Vampire* . . . vampire plays of every kind from the most luridly sensational to the most farcically ridiculous pressed on to the boards. A contemporary critic cries: 'There is not a theatre in Paris without its Vampire! At the Porte-Sainte-Martin we have *Le Vampire*; at the Vaudeville *Le Vampire* again; at the Variétés *Les Trois Vampires ou le clair de la lune*.

In the last of these plays, a romantic farce, a protective father and keen Byron reader assumes that the young men who are in pursuit of his daughters and his maid must be vampires because they loiter around his gardens at night. Other productions of 1820 include *Encore un Vampire, Les Etrennes d'un Vampire, and Cadet Buteux, vampire* . . . It was this sudden Parisian fad for all things vampiric that inspired Anne Rice to imagine a Théâtre des Vampires for her debut novel *Interview with the Vampire*.

Nodier's play was soon adapted for the London stage as *The Vampire; or, the Bride of the Isles*, by a somewhat reluctant James Robinson Planché (who thought that the Scottish setting was ridiculous, and would laugh at all the Caledonian flummery, and particularly at Ruthven's first appearance in kilt and tam-o'-shanter). It opened at the English Opera House (later the Lyceum) on 9 August 1820. The production was notable for its special effects, and so can be seen as initiating the convention that vampiric spectacles should be crammed with visual tricks and treats. The most important of them was a trapdoor, which allowed the actor playing Ruthven to disappear in a puff of smoke; to this day, such gadgets are still sometimes referred to by stagehands as 'vampire traps'.

. . . AND THE OPERA

The next major metamorphosis of Nodier's play was into an opera, Heinrich August Marschner's *Der Vampyr* (1828). Marschner's librettist was Wilhelm August Wohlbrück, who adapted it from a German version of Nodier's play by Heinrich Ludwig Ritter. Ritter had taken a number of liberties with his source, especially with its conclusion, but it is recognizable as the same yarn, with Lord Ruthven once again the hero/villain. With the possible exception of August Enna's *Lamia*, this is the only major vampire opera composed before Alva Henderson's *Nosferatu* (see Chapter Five) was published in the twenty-first century. There are records of an earlier opera by the

Italian composer Silvestro di Palma, *I Vampiri*, produced in Naples in 1800, but little is known of this work. Marschner's work did have an immediate successor, though: a now-forgotten production of the same name by Peter Joseph von Lindpainter (words by Cäsar Max Heigel) which also adheres to Nodier's version, though it changes the central character's name to Graf Aubri.

Der Vampyr premiered in Leipzig on 28 March 1828, and was such a hit that there was an almost immediate demand for a British adaptation. Once again, Planché accepted the task of translating the work, but this time he insisted on having a much freer hand, shifting the action away from vampire-free Scotland and to somewhere which now seems far more suitable:

> I was engaged to write the English libretto and consequently laid the scene of action in Hungary, where the superstition exists to this day, substituted for a Scotch chieftain a Wallachian Boyard, and in many other respects improved upon my earlier version.

'A Wallachian Boyard', indeed? Next stop, Transylvania. (And see the works of Karl Marx, below.) *Der Vampyr* has been revived a number of times, and was transformed into a strange television drama series – *The Vampyr: A Soap Opera* – in 1992, written by Charles Hart and directed by Nigel Finch of the *Arena* team. The final, late flowering of the Ruthven/Nodier story was a melodrama by Alexandre Dumas in 1851. Dumas had watched a revival of the Nodier play twenty-eight years earlier, and wrote a detailed account of his experience.

Still Undead after All These Years: the Modern Vampire Byron

Byron, both as a supernatural creature and in his mortal form, continues to stalk the pages of vampire fiction. Major examples include:

Tim Powers, The Stress of Her Regard (1989). It features not only Byron but also Keats, Shelley and Polidori; Powers's earlier novel, *The Anubis Gates* (1983), also includes Byron, here as a brainwashed assassin with a mission to kill King George.

Tom Holland, The Vampyre: Being the True Pilgrimage of George Gordon, Sixth Lord Byron (1995). The title spells out the basic premise, though in the USA it appeared under the more ambiguous title *Lord of the Dead*. In Britain, the sequel (1996) was entitled *Supping with Panthers*; in the USA, it was called *Slave of My Thirst*.

'Lord Ruthven', meanwhile, is a major character in Kim Newman's brilliant *Anno Dracula* series; see Chapter Five.

OTHER NINETEENTH-CENTURY VAMPIRE SIGHTINGS

In addition to all the more famous vampires considered here, there were a fair number of less celebrated undead manifestations in nineteenth-century European literature. Here are some minor landmarks – or tombstones – of the developing genre. Note that in some instances – Edgar Allan Poe's 'Berenice', for instance – the theme of vampirism is not directly named; and that in others, the vampire is less a tangible being than a malignant, invisible force.

✝ John Tieck, 'Wake Not The Dead' (circa 1800; first published in English in 1823).

✝ Heinrich von Kleist, *The Marquise of O . . .* (1805).

✝ E. T. A. Hoffmann, *The Serapion Brotherhood* (1820), especially 'Aurelia'.

✝ Prosper Mérimée, *La Gazla* (1827).

✝ Edgar Allen Poe, 'Berenice' (1833).

✝ Nikolai Gogol, *Viy* (1835).

✝ Théophile Gautier, *La Morte amoureuse* (1836).

✝ Alexei Tolstoy, *Upyr* ('Vampire') and *The Family of the Vourdalak* (early 1840s; published 1884).

✝ Alexandre Dumas, *The Pale-Faced Lady* (1848).

✝ Fitzgerald O'Brien, 'What Was It?' (1859).

✝ Algernon Charles Swinburne, *Chastelard* (1865) – the vampire is Mary, Queen of Scots.

✝ Comte de Lautréamont (aka Isidore Ducasse), *Les Chants de Maldoror* (1868); a favourite of the Surrealists.

✝ Eliza Lynn Linton, 'The Fate of Madame Cabanel' (1880).

✝ Guy de Maupassant, *Le Horla* (1887).

✝ Ambrose Bierce, 'The Death of Halpin Frayser' (1893).

✝ Eric, Count Stenbock, *A True Story of a Vampire* (1894).

✝ 'X. L.' (aka Julian Osgood Field), *A Kiss of Judas* (1894).

✝ Mary Elizabeth Braddon, *Good Lady Ducayne* (1896).

The Vampire Quartet

In the nineteenth century, there were four basic vamp archetypes:

✝ The Satanic Lord (Polidori and derivatives).

✝ The Fatal Woman or *Femme Fatale* (Tieck, Hoffmann, Gautier, Baudelaire, Swinburne, Le Fanu).

✝ The Unseen Force (O'Brien, de Maupassant).

✝ The Folkloric Vampire (Mérimée, Gogol, Tolstoy, Turgenev, Linton).

For more details, see Christopher Frayling's survey *Vampyres: Lord Byron to Count Dracula* (1993).

VICTORIAN VAMPS

At least five vampire dramas were staged in Victorian London, most notably Dion Boucicault's *The Vampire: A Phantasm in Three Dramas* (1852). Boucicault (1820–90) was one of the most successful theatrical entrepreneurs of his day. He wrote the play with the great stage star Edmund Kean in mind, but when the actor refused the lead part, he took it himself. The play did not do well at first, and in the course of the next few years Boucicault rewrote it thoroughly as *The Phantom*. One of his alterations was to rename his vampire, so that Alan Raby became – what invention! – Sir Alan Ruthven. *The Phantom* came to London in 1861 and fared much better than its prototype. It was later one of the various targets of Gilbert and Sullivan in their spoof *Ruddigore* (1887) – which, by the way, includes a character called Sir Ruthven Murgatroyd.

For further information on this relatively unknown phenomenon of stage vampirism, see Roxanne Stuart, *Stage Blood: Vampires in the Nineteenth-Century Stage* (1984).

THE PENNY-DREADFUL VAMPIRE: ENTER VARNEY

The first full-length (and then some) vampire novel in English was published as a series of pamphlets – 'penny dreadfuls', as these cheap fictions were popularly known – from 1846–7: *Varney the Vampire; or, the Feast of Blood*, by James Malcolm Rymer, a former civil engineer turned indefatigable hack. (The widespread assumption that it had been written by the author of *Sweeney Todd*, Thomas Preskett Prest, was definitively proved wrong in 1963, though plenty of books continue to identify Prest as the author.) It ran, eventually, to 220 chapters across 868 double-columned pages, and was numbingly repetitious.

Heavily dependent on Polidori's simple plot, it takes as its villain one Sir Francis Varney, of Ratford Hall, Yorkshire, and for his principal victims the Bannerworth family. Rymer is not very good at keeping a grip on his continuity, and though the novel appears to be set mainly in the early eighteenth century there are occasional references to the Napoleonic Wars of the early nineteenth century. Varney, who loathes and curses his condition, appears to have become a vampire at the time of the Civil War, when he betrayed a Royalist to Cromwell, then accidentally killed his own son. Eventually, Varney decides to end his long misery by throwing himself into Vesuvius.

While not exactly fine writing, *Varney* handed the genre some enduringly useful props: his fangs ('tusk-like teeth'), the tell-tale puncture marks on his victims' necks, his hypnotic powers and his immense strength. And there are a half-dozen or so other small details which eventually found their way into Stoker's *Dracula* . . .

THE BRONTË VAMPIRE

Jane Eyre has suffered a terrible fright: some nocturnal visitor to her bedroom. The next day she tries to explain to Mr Rochester what she has seen. Rochester suggests that ghosts are usually pale, but she replies, 'This, sir, was purple: the lips were swelled and dark: the brow furrowed; the black eyebrows wide raised over the blood-shot eyes. Shall I tell you of what it reminded me? . . . Of that foul German spectre – the Vampyre' (*Jane Eyre*, 1847).

It is in fact the first Mrs Rochester. But note the incriminating details; and the fact that, half a century before Stoker, it is still Germany, not Transylvania, that is viewed as the home of vampirism.

THE BAUDELAIREAN VAMPIRE

This brisk survey would not be complete without mention of the significant fact that one of the nineteenth century's greatest masterpieces of poetry, Baudelaire's *Les Fleurs du Mal* (*Flowers of Evil*) – a book which is sometimes said to have opened the door to modern poetry, in all languages – contains two verses on vampiric themes: '*Le Vampire*' and '*Les Metamorphoses du vampire*'. Or, rather, it would have contained them had the book not fallen foul of the law and been censored.

In the spirit of Keats's *La Belle Dame sans Merci*, Baudelaire's vampires are female. Oh, yes: and fatal.

Le Vampire

Toi qui, comme un coup de couteau,
Dans mon coeur plaintif es entrée;
Toi qui, forte comme un troupeau
De démons, vins, folle et parée,

De mon esprit humilié
Faire ton lit et ton domaine;
—Infâme à qui je suis lié
Comme un forçat à la chaîne,

Comme au jeu le joueur têtu,
Comme à la bouteille l'ivrogne,
Comme aux vermines la charogne,
—Maudite, maudite sois-tu!

J'ai prié le glaive rapide
De conquérir ma liberté
Et j'ai dit au poison perfide
De secourir ma lâcheté.

Hélas! le poison et le glaive
M'ont pris en dédain et m'ont dit:
'Tu n'es pas digne qu'on t'enlève
A ton esclavage maudit,

Imbécile!—de son empire
Si nos efforts te délivraient,
Tes baisers ressusciteraient
Le cadavre de ton vampire!'

Here is a literal translation into free verse:

The Vampire

You who, like the stab of a knife,
Entered into my plaintive heart;
You who, strong as a troupe
Of demons, came wild and ready.

Make my humiliated spirit
Into your bed and your domain;
—Infamous woman to whom I'm bound
Like the prisoner to his chain.

Like the stubborn gambler to his game,
Like the drunkard to his bottle,
Like maggots in carrion flesh,
—May you be cursed, cursed!

I begged the swift blade
To win my liberty for me
And I told wicked poison
To help my cowardice.

Alas! The poison and the blade
Held me in disdain and said:
'You are not worthy of being released
From your accursed slavery,

Fool! Even if our efforts were
To deliver you from her empire,
Your kisses would resuscitate
The corpse of your vampire!'

THE ORIENTALIST VAMPIRE

In 1870, the great Victorian explorer, linguist, soldier and diplomat Sir Richard Burton (1821–90) published *Vikram and the Vampire*. Burton had come across the tales of King Vikram – loosely speaking, a sort of Indian counterpart to King Arthur – in a set of manuscripts which told of his exploits, as narrated by a *vetala* – an Indian vampire. Burton's renderings of some of these adventures have disappointingly little to attract modern vampire fans, though the author was fond of saying that the book was a major contribution to the genre. He more than earns his place in the annals, though, for his possible role as an original for the appearance of Dracula. Bram Stoker met Burton in the course of his work as manager of the Lyceum Theatre (the showplace for the most famous actor of his day, Sir Henry Irving) and was struck by his features: 'Burton's face seemed to lengthen when he laughed; the upper lip rising instinctively and showing the right canine tooth. This was always a characteristic of his enjoyment.'

ENTER THE LESBIAN VAMPIRE

By far the most important vampire fiction in the eighty-odd years between Polidori's tale and Stoker's novel is a short story by Sheridan Le Fanu, first published in 1872: *Carmilla*. The lesbian theme in vampire fiction was not entirely novel – see Coleridge's *Christabel* – but Le Fanu gave it definitive form, and it has been a palpable presence in the literature ever since.

The story is narrated by Laura, the lonely daughter of a retired English gentleman who had worked in the Austrian civil service; at the time the narrative begins, Laura is nineteen, but she spends a while recalling a curious and disturbing dream she had when she was six, in which a mysterious female presence slipped into her bed, hurting her as if with twin needles. The action proper begins when

Laura and her father witness a coach accident. The rather haughty lady who owns the carriage insists that she must carry on her journey, but agrees to leave her daughter Carmilla behind as a companion for Laura. To Laura's astonishment, Carmilla exactly resembles the woman from her dream. The two girls are soon launched on an intense friendship, but matters grow sinister. First there are reports of death in the district; then terrible things start to happen at night. Laura thinks she sees a giant cat prowling in her bedroom one night; then she falls increasingly ill, drifting into a state of lassitude.

Eventually, with the help of a retired general whose own daughter has fallen victim to the same kind of nocturnal malaise and died, Laura and her father come to see that Carmilla is a vampire – in fact, Countess Mircalla Karnstein, who died 150 years earlier. (The potentially interesting idea that vampires must always present themselves under their real name or an anagrammatical variant was not taken up in the subsequent literature, unless one counts all the Alucards who appear from 1936 onwards.) Laura does not witness the horrible finale, but learns later that Carmilla was tracked to her tomb, found floating in seven inches of fresh blood, and seen off by being decapitatated.

How 'lesbian' is *Carmilla*? Within the limits of literary decorum, quite strongly. At one point, Carmilla is described as:

> gazing in my face with languid and burning eyes, and breathing so fast that her dress rose and fell with tumultuous respiration. It was like the ardour of a lover; it embarrassed me; it was hateful and yet overpowering; and with gloating eyes she drew me to her, and her hot lips travelled along my cheek in kisses; and she would whisper, almost in sobs, 'You are mine, you shall be mine, and you and I are one forever . . . '

Bewildered, Laura starts to wonder whether Carmilla might not actually be an ingenious boy seducer, dressed up in frocks.

Some films based on *Carmilla* include:

✝ *Vampyr* (1931, directed by Carl Theodor Dreyer). A very loose adaptation; see Chapter Four.

✝ *Blood and Roses* (1961, directed by Roger Vadim; otherwise *Et Mourir de plaisir*).

And then a highly successful Hammer Films 'Karnstein' trilogy:

✝ *The Vampire Lovers* (1970, directed by Roy Ward Baker).

✝ *Lust for a Vampire* (1971, directed by Jimmy Sangster).

✝ *Twins of Evil* (1971, directed by John Hough).

✝ *The Blood-Spattered Bride* (1972, directed by Vincente Aranda; otherwise *La Novia ensangrentada*).

✝ *The Evil of Dracula* (1974, directed by Michio Yamamoto).

✝ *Captain Kronos: Vampire Hunter* (1974, directed by Brian Clemens).

✝ *Carmilla* (various TV films: UK 1966, Spain 1987, USA 1989 . . .).

There was also a stage musical version of *Carmilla* (1970), devised by Wilford Leach for the La MaMa Experimental Theatre Club, New York; and a comic book (1968), published outside the conventions of the Comics Code by the Warren Publishing Company.

✝HE FANGS OF ✝HE MONA LISA

From Walter Pater's *Studies in the Art of the Renaissance*, published in 1873:

She is older than the rocks among which she sits; like the vampire, she has been dead many times, and learned the secrets of the grave; and has been a diver in deep seas, and keeps their fallen day about her; and trafficked for strange webs with Eastern merchants and, as Leda, was the mother of Helen of

Troy, and, as Saint Anne, the Mother of Mary; and all this has been to her but as the sounds of lyres and flutes, and lives only in the delicacy with which it has moulded the changing lineaments, and tinged the eyelids and the hands . . .

THE PEOPLE'S BLOOD IS BRIGHTEST RED: THE MARXIST VAMPIRE

By the time Karl Marx wrote the first volume of *Das Kapital* in 1867, all Europe knew what vampires were, so that the metaphor of vampirism came readily to his pen. In the English translation, *Capital* (1887; Volume One, Chapter 10), the crucial sentence reads thus:

> Capital is dead labour, which, vampire-like, lives only by sucking living labour, and lives the more, the more labour it sucks.

This passage is frequently cited by economists and vampirologists alike; but it was the cultural historian Professor Sir Christopher Frayling who first spotted that the same chapter of *Capital* includes a reference to 'the Wallachian Boyard' – that is, to Vlad the Impaler.

THE FIN-DE-SIÈCLE VAMPIRE

In the final years before Stoker changed everything, most of the vampires that haunted Europe were female, beautiful, young (in appearance) and deadly. They were literal *femmes fatales*. Here, for instance, is Arthur Symons, 'The Vampire':

> *Intolerable woman, where's the name*
> *For your insane complexity of shame?*
> *Vampire! white bloodless creature of the night,*
> *Whose lust of blood has blanched her chill veins white,*

Veins fed with moonlight over dead men's tombs;
Whose eyes remember many martyrdoms,
So that their depths, whose depths cannot be found,
Are shadowed pools in which a soul lies drowned;
Who would fain have pity, but she may not rest
Till she has sucked a man's heart from his breast,
And drained his life-blood from him, vein, by vein,
And seen his eyes grow brighter for the pain,
And his lips sigh her name with his last breath,
As the man swoons ecstatically on death.

This woman's sisters were legion. From their ranks issued the most famous she-vampire of the day.

MR KIPLING'S EXCEEDINGLY INFLUENTIAL VAMPIRE

In 1897, the year of *Dracula*, Rudyard Kipling published these verses under the title 'The Vampire':

A fool there was and he made his prayer
(Even as you and I!)
To a rag and a bone and a hank of hair
(We called her the woman who did not care)
But the fool he called her his lady fair –
(Even as you and I!)

Oh, the years we waste and the tears we waste
And the work of our head and hand,
Belong to the woman who did not know
(And now we know that she never could know)
And did not understand!

A fool there was and his goods he spent
(Even as you and I!)
Honour and faith and a sure intent
(And it wasn't the least what the lady meant)
But a fool must follow his natural bent
(Even as you and I!)

Oh, the toil we lost and the spoil we lost
And the excellent things we planned
Belonged to the woman who didn't know why
(And now we know that she never knew why)
And did not understand!

The fool was stripped to his foolish hide
(Even as you and I!)
Which she might have seen when she threw him aside –
(But it isn't on record the lady tried)
So some of him lived but the most of him died –
(Even as you and I)

And it isn't the shame and it isn't the blame
That stings like a white-hot brand –
It's coming to know that she never knew why
(Seeing at last she could never know why)
And never could understand.

Kipling wrote this poem as a kind of advertisement for a painting, *The Vampire*, by his cousin Philip Burne-Jones, a sensational, deliciously erotic work which – inverting the composition of Fuseli's *The Nightmare* (see Chapter One) – showed a woman in a flowing gown on top of a swooning, bare-chested, possibly dead man from whom she has clearly drained some vital force. Part of the painting's scandal, which increased when it was shipped to America and shown there, was that the woman in the painting was obviously based on Mrs Patrick Campbell, the actress and idol of the masses.

Burne-Jones's painting arrived in America just as the cinema was taking off, and early producers took notice. Inspired by the appearance of the woman as well as the erotic theme, they produced lots of films about the figure of the 'vamp' – of whom the most famous was the actress Theda Bara, née Theodosia Goodman (1889–1955; the stage name is an anagram of 'Arab Death'). A play inspired by Burne-Jones's *The Vampire* was produced in 1909; the screen version, *A Fool There Was* (1915), made Bara a star.

†HR€€

†H€ BLOOD COUN†

*All about Dracula, and **Dracula***

In the early months of the year 1897, everything changed. Bram Stoker published *Dracula*.

Dracula is to vampires what *The Origin of Species* is to the theory of evolution, what *Das Kapital* is to Marxism, what 'A Study in Scarlet' is to detective fiction. It set all the basic supernatural rules, all the narrative conventions of menace, chase and redemption. It even determined some of the conventional sets and trappings. There have, since 1897, been scarier vampire novels, as well as vampire novels that are better written, more ingenious, more tragic, more profound, funnier and more poetic. None of this matters. Just as Western philosophy has been described as a series of footnotes to Plato, all subsequent vampire fiction is a series of footnotes to *Dracula*. Here goes.

†H€ S†ORY

The story is so well known, such an indispensable part of popular mythology, that almost everyone thinks they know it, even if they have never actually read Stoker's novel. In broad terms, this is probably true; but since none of the famous movies based on the book has been particularly faithful – the closest dramatization to date has probably been the BBC television production of 1977, starring Louis

Jourdan – Stoker's original design has become blurred and distorted. And those who have read the novel will be aware of a trickier, more subtle kind of distortion, due to the book's unusual form.

Stoker presents his novel as a series of found documents (he borrowed the structure from Wilkie Collins; see below) – diaries, letters, clips from newspapers and magazines, and recordings on a phonograph. This is a form well suited to his flesh-creeping ends, since it appears to ground all of the supernatural goings-on in everyday reality, and also because it means that the reader enjoys the delightful agony of knowing that the characters, who cannot see the bigger picture, are wandering unwittingly into danger or doom. (We thus becomes like children at the pantomime, screaming, 'Look behind you!' as the Monster creeps up on the Heroine.) But the fact that there is no omniscient or reliable narrator to tie up all the ends for us means that the story is full of gaps, ambiguities and areas of mystery, most of which are inevitably tidied away in summary. What, for example, is the origin of Dracula's hold over Renfield? What brings Dracula to Whitby at exactly the moment Lucy and Mina happen to be there? Screenwriters have often struggled to plug these narrative gaps.

With that caveat in mind, it goes something like this:

Jonathan Harker, a young, recently qualified solicitor, has been dispatched by his employer to the wild regions of the Carpathians to consult with an elderly aristocrat, Count Dracula, who has recently been buying a number of properties in England. Despite the warnings of some superstitious locals, and the ominous spookiness of his coach ride through the Borgo Pass with a mysterious, preternaturally strong driver, Harker is initially quite taken with Dracula's old-world thoughtfulness and courtesy. Gradually, though, he starts to find the Count more and more sinister, and to realize that he is in effect being held prisoner in Dracula's castle. After a half-terrifying, half-arousing encounter with three voluptuous women (who are, we realize, about to devour him when Dracula angrily intervenes), Harker concludes that Dracula means to kill him. He resolves to escape from the castle, even if it costs him his life.

Back in England, Harker's fiancée Mina Murray, an assistant schoolmistress, is in correspondence with her old schoolfriend, the much richer and grander Lucy Westenra, a beautiful nineteen-year-old. Lucy is excited by having had three proposals of marriage on the same day: one from Dr John Seward, a talented young psychiatrist who runs his own asylum; one from a wealthy Texan, Quincey Morris; and one from the Honourable Arthur Holmwood – the candidate she picks. Seward, to soothe his broken heart, throws himself into his work, and becomes increasingly interested in the case of a bizarre patient called Renfield, who likes to catch and eat flies and spiders.

Mina and Lucy travel to Whitby on a short holiday; while they are there, Lucy begins to act rather strangely, and resumes a childhood habit of walking in her sleep. Then comes a violent storm, which brings ashore a ship, the *Demeter*, crewless save for its dead captain who has lashed himself to the wheel. His fragmentary log tells of terrible happenings en route, and the death or disappearance, one by one, of all hands. Reports say that a giant dog jumped off the ship, whose hold proves to contain nothing save fifty boxes of earth.

Lucy becomes ever more restless and troubled; Mina is worried both by this and by the unaccountable lack of letters from her fiancé. Finally, she hears from a nun in Budapest, who explains that Jonathan has been found, desperately ill from 'brain fever', but is slowly recovering. Mina immediately sets off for Budapest, where she and Jonathan are promptly married. Lucy moves back to London, but grows more and more sickly (and, as if in parallel, Renfield grows more and more crazed). Arthur Holmwood calls Seward in to examine her, and Seward, puzzled by her unusual symptoms, which include vast and inexplicable blood loss, writes to Amsterdam to summon help from his old mentor, the polymathic Professor Abraham Van Helsing. Van Helsing soon discovers – but does not immediately explain to his new friends – that Lucy has been the victim of nocturnal attacks by a vampire.

Lucy's condition worsens, despite Van Helsing's repeated transfusions of blood from willing male donors. One night, a wolf, apparently escaped from London Zoo – a 'Berserker', or, as one cockney zoo-keeper calls him, a 'Bersicker' – attacks the Westenra house, and the shock causes Lucy's invalid mother to die. (Arthur's father has also died, so the young man has inherited the title Lord Godalming.) Then Lucy dies; or rather, as Van Helsing knows, passes into un-death. Shortly after her burial, newspapers report a series of child abductions in and near Hampstead Heath, and sightings of a 'Bloofer' ('beautiful', as lisped by a child) Lady; Van Helsing recognizes the dreadful signs, and, despite the initial outrage and disgust of Seward and the others, leads them to Lucy's tomb, where Holmwood stakes her.

Jonathan and Mina, back in Britain, spot a man who, though seeming many years younger than the elderly creature in Transylvania, is obviously Dracula himself. It becomes clear that the Count is at the root of all this evil – it is he who exercises an uncanny hold over Renfield – and must be hunted down and destroyed. The allies manage to track down most of Dracula's earth-filled boxes in their various locations and, using fragments of the Host, render them useless for him. But Dracula counter-attacks; he kills Renfield, and then finds Mina, bites her, and forces her to sup some of his own blood. The friends interrupt him, and he flees, but the damage is done: Mina is turning into a vampire, and her flesh burns when the Host is applied.

From here on, the action is mostly a chase. Dracula manages to find a ship to take him on the first stage of his journey home. The allies follow; Van Helsing takes Mina with him, because she now has a kind of telepathic link with the Count which gives at least some information as to his actions. Eventually, after a long race against time, Van Helsing and Mina reach Castle Dracula, where the professor hacks the three vampire women to pieces. The final act takes the form of a race against sunset, as Dracula's coach, guarded by a band of hired gypsy warriors, brings him back to his lair. But Godalming, Harker and Quincey overpower the guard; Harker slashes Dracula's throat with a kukri knife, and Morris plunges his bowie knife into the vampire's heart. Dracula explodes into dust. As he disintegrates, the scar on Mina's brow vanishes; she is clean again. Quincey, wounded in his side, dies happily.

A brief coda, written by Harker seven years later, explains that Mina and he now have a son, named after all the men in the band but usually called Quincey. Seward and Goldalming have also made happy marriages. The events are now so much in the past that the Harkers have recently been able to revisit Transylvania, and feel no pang of horror.

WHAT DOES DRACULA LOOK LIKE?

According to Jonathan Harker, at first, it's like this:

> Within, stood a tall old man, clean-shaven save for a long white moustache, and clad in black from head to foot, without a single speck of colour anywhere . . .

Note that there is no mention of the trademark cloak or evening dress, which were introduced in the earliest productions of the stage play and then made famous by Lugosi in the Tod Browning film. Very few films have given Dracula a moustache or beard, one notable exception being the 1968 Thames Television drama starring Denholm Elliott.

> His face was a strong – a very strong – aquiline, with high bridge of the thin nose and peculiarly arched nostrils, with lofty domed forehead, and hair growing scantily around the temples but

profusely elsewhere. His eyebrows were very massive, almost meeting over the nose, and with bushy hair that seemed to curl in its own profusion. The mouth, so far as I could see it under the heavy moustache, was fixed and rather cruel-looking, with peculiarly sharp white teeth; these protruded over the lips, whose remarkable ruddiness showed astonishing vitality in a man of his years. For the rest, his ears were pale, and at the tops extremely pointed; the chin was broad and strong, and the cheeks firm though thin. The general effect was one of extraordinary pallor . . .

Hitherto I had noticed the backs of his hands as they lay on his knees in the firelight, and they had seemed rather white and fine, but seeing them now close to me, I could not but notice that they were rather coarse – broad, squat fingers. Strange to say, there were hairs in the centre of the palm. The nails were long and fine, and cut to a sharp point . . .

Harker also goes on to mention that Dracula has very bad breath.

But this detailed description only tells part of the story, for Dracula is a shape-shifter. A vampire who can turn into a wolf, a bat, or sheer mist has little difficulty in making changes to his apparently human form. When in a rage, his usually blue eyes glow red like the fires of Hell. He can readily make himself look much younger, especially after feeding, when his white hair changes to an 'iron-grey'.

THE VAMPIRE RULE BOOK

Bram Stoker established almost all of the fundamental traits of the vampire as we know it, plus a few that have fallen by the way over the years. He derived his facts from more or less authentic folklore (his primary source was Emily Gerard's travel book about Transylvania, *The*

Land Beyond the Forest, 1885), as well as drawing on details from previous imaginative literature, and adding elements from his own invention.

Van Helsing gives a long lecture on vampiric strengths and weaknesses in Chapter XVIII (with a few supplementary comments elsewhere). He begins like this:

> The vampire live on, and cannot die by mere passing of the time; he can flourish when that he can fatten on the blood of the living . . . he can even grow younger . . . his vital faculties grow strenuous, and seem as though they refresh themselves when his special pabulum is plenty. But he cannot flourish without this diet; he eat not as others.

Paraphrasing from Van Helsing's quaintly fractured English, and supplementing his wisdom with observations from the rest of the novel, we may arrive at the following set of criteria.

The vampire:

✝ Can survive for many centuries, perhaps forever, unless killed in the approved fashion.

✝ Subsists wholly on (human) blood.

✝ Is immensely strong ('so strong in person as twenty men') and cunning.

✝ Can control the weather ('the storm, the fog, the thunder').

✝ Is a necromancer ('He have still the aids of necromancy, which is, as his etymology imply, the divination by the dead, and all the dead that he can come nigh to are for him at command').

✝ Can control some animals ('all the meaner things: the rat, and the owl, and the bat – the moth, and the fox, and the wolf').

✝ Can vanish at will.

✝ Can exercise a kind of hypnotic control over his victims, both at short range and over great distances.

✝ Can read the minds of those with whom he has established some bond.

✝ Casts no reflection ('he make in the mirror no reflect').

✝ Casts no shadow (though some of the creepiest effects in Dracula films, above all Murnau's *Nosferatu* (1922), have come from making play with the fiend's menacing shadow).

✝ Can transform himself into a wolf, a bat, or a mist, or turn into 'elemental dust' carried on moonlight.

✝ Can make himself so small that he can slide in through the narrowest gaps.

✝ Can see in the dark ('no small power this, in a world which is one half shut from the light').

✝ May not enter any building unless first invited by an inmate.

✝ Loses most or all of his supernatural powers in the daytime.

✝ Can only shape-shift at noon, sunrise and sunset.

✝ Usually sleeps during the daytime, in a coffin containing earth from his home (but, note, is not much harmed by sunlight. The idea that vampires burn, crumble and die when exposed to daylight begins only a quarter of a century later, with Murnau's *Nosferatu* in 1922).

✝ Can only cross running water at the slack or flood of the tide (in some vampire films, the creatures can be killed or at least wounded with running water).

✝ Is repelled by the crucifix and the Eucharistic wafer and, by implication, all other sacred things.

✝ Is burned by contact with holy things.

✝ Is repelled by garlic (but also the by wild rose, and the mountain ash: most subsequent vampire tales have forgotten these, though in *Salem's Lot* the vampire hunters also provide themselves with hawthorn. A branch of wild rose placed on his coffin will keep him trapped inside).

✝ Must be destroyed by being staked, then decapitated, and the mouth stuffed with garlic; or by a 'sacred bullet' fired into his coffin (what makes a bullet 'sacred'? Presumably, being blessed by an obliging priest. Some writers of vampire fiction have assumed that the undead, like werewolves, can be destroyed by silver bullets, but this is a much more recent convention).

✝ Can create new vampires by having the victim suck his own blood.

WHO WAS S✝OKER?

In his lifetime, Abraham 'Bram' Stoker (1847–1912) was much better known as the manager of the actor Sir Henry Irving than as a man of letters in his own right, though he was the author of about eighteen books, including several novels – notably *The Jewel of the Seven Stars* (1903) and *The Lair of the White Worm* (1911), both of which inspired films. He also wrote a number of non-fiction books, including a two-volume memorial to his late employer, *The Personal Reminiscences of Henry Irving*. It would have amazed his contemporaries to learn that Stoker's claim to immortality would rest on the spooky book he published in 1897.

Stoker, the third of seven children, was born and raised in Dublin. He was a sickly child, and spent his earliest years bedridden with what may have been a form of hysterical paralysis, from which he made a near-miraculous recovery at the age of seven. Once in his teens, Bram became a more than passable athlete. He entered Trinity College at sixteen, and graduated with a bachelor's degree in science in 1870, having in the meantime been president of the Philosophical Society (he sponsored the membership of his friend Oscar Wilde, whom he continued to know well for years afterwards) and auditor of the Historical Society. Among the books he seems to have read during these formative years was Sheridan Le Fanu's gothic novella *Carmilla*.

On graduation, he joined the Irish civil service, but soon began moonlighting as a theatre critic for the *Dublin Evening Mail*. He also became part-time editor of a small newspaper, which folded shortly afterwards, and began to write his earliest fiction – a horror tale, 'The Chain of Destiny', was published in 1875. He also wrote a book entitled *The Duties of Clerks of Petty Sessions in Ireland*, which is said to be not nearly as exciting as it sounds.

In 1878, Irving took over management of the Lyceum Theatre in London, and invited Stoker – whose fervent but penetrating review of one of his performances as Hamlet on an Irish tour had first caught his attention – to join the company as manager. It was the start of a close collaboration between the two men which lasted for twenty-seven years, until Irving's death in 1905. Stoker worked prodigiously hard for his boss, and was well paid for his troubles, but he still found enough spare time to marry – also in 1878 – a famous Dublin beauty, Florence Anne Lemon Balcombe (Oscar Wilde had also courted her for a time), to sire a son, Irving Noel Stoker, to acquire a smart house in Chelsea, and to publish his first major works of fiction – now mainly forgotten. He began piecing together the earliest materials for his vampire book in March 1890, and continued writing it on a holiday in Whitby that summer. His working titles included *The Un-Dead* and *The Dead Un-Dead* and, after a while, *Count Dracula*. The book took seven years to complete. It was published by Constable in a bright yellow cover – yellow was the fashionably decadent colour of the 1890s – in May 1897.

Wanting to establish a dramatic copyright for the work, Stoker staged a long public reading of a roughly adapted version of the book at the Lyceum on 18 May 1897; thus, the date on which his vampire first took the stage. It ran to forty-seven scenes across five acts; the story goes that Sir Henry Irving eavesdropped on proceedings for a few minutes. Asked what he thought, he replied, *'Dreadful!'*

After Irving's death, Stoker suffered from a stroke and then developed Bright's disease, a condition of the kidneys. He was able to continue writing, but without a regular day job he and Florence soon became impoverished. His death on 12 April 1912 (the same week the *Titanic* sank) was ascribed to 'locomotor ataxia' – generally understood to be a euphemism for tertiary syphilis, though some biographers have disputed this claim. Florence lived on for many years until 1937, publishing a collection of Stoker's short fiction, including the enigmatic 'Dracula's Guest' in 1914, and waging an eight-year copyright war against Prana-Film for their obvious plagiarism of Stoker's work in Murnau's *Nosferatu*.

Stoker, a burly, bearded man, wrote endless letters for his employer, sometimes as many as fifty a day, but left few documents of his inner life, and though he was drawn to supernatural subjects, there is little to hint that he had any belief in occult phenomena. (A rumour that he joined a celebrated occultist group, the Hermetic Order of the Golden Dawn, remains unsubstantiated, if tantalizing. If he did join, a possible sponsor was Constance Wilde, Oscar's wife, an active member of the group.) Since 1984, when Christopher Craft published his essay 'Kiss Me With Those Red Lips: Gender and Inversion in *Dracula*', it has often been speculated that Stoker was homosexual, and that *Dracula* is a lightly disguised treatment of gay themes. (In his working notes, Stoker wrote out the memorable line Dracula uses to shoo his Brides away from Harker: 'This man is mine!')

It's possible. Consider that, at the age of twenty-four, young Stoker wrote an almost startlingly effusive letter to Walt Whitman, the great – and gay – American poet: 'How sweet a thing it is for a strong healthy man with a woman's eyes and a child's wishes [Stoker meant himself] to feel that he can speak so to a man who can be if he wishes father and brother and wife to his soul.' The two men eventually met when Stoker accompanied the Lyceum troupe on an American tour. And what about Stoker's feelings for Irving? After one of the first dinners he shared with his boss-to-be, Stoker collapsed in a hysterical fit, so wrought up was he by a monologue the actor had just recited for his benefit. For years to come, contemporaries commented on how deeply Stoker submerged his life in that of Irving. In that relatively innocent age, even after the Wilde trial, no one saw anything queer in stating, as they often did, that Bram's true marriage was not to Florence but to Sir Henry.

Incidentally, Irving is often cited as one of the possible sources of the Count's physical appearance and mannerisms.

LITERARY AND PHILOSOPHICAL INSPIRATIONS

Wilkie Collins, *The Woman in White* (1860). Stoker planned from the very beginning to present his tale in an up-to-date variant of that traditional literary form, the epistolary novel; and the vast commercial success of Wilkie Collins's book showed that there was still plenty of life in the old convention.

George du Maurier, *Trilby* (1894). (And note this date. Though some commentators have stated that *Trilby* must have been a decisive influence on *Dracula*, Stoker had already been at work on his novel for four years.) This is the tale of a young artist's model who falls under the hypnotic influence of Svengali, an impressario and, so to say, psychic vampire. When she is in a trance state, Trilby becomes a wonderful singer, and gains fame as 'La Svengali'. Svengali eventually dies, and Trilby appears to be freed, but the mere sight of a picture of her former manipulator sends her back into a singing trance, and she, too, dies. Du Maurier's book, not much read these days, was one of the decade's best-sellers. Svengali, we should also note, is a Jewish villain, and in some respects Dracula resembles the stereotypical Jew of stage and fiction – especially Shylock as played, numberless times, by Irving.

John William Polidori, 'The Vampyre', and other Gothic or generally spooky fictions, including *Carmilla* by Sheridan Le Fanu (certainly), *Varney the Vampire* by James Malcolm Rymer (almost certainly), and a short story called 'The Mysterious Stranger' (first published anonymously in 1860; the author has never been identified), which features a 'Count Azzo von Klatka' (probably).

Lord Byron, 'The Giaour' (1813; see p.37). In Chapter XIII, Dr Seward makes an unacknowledged Byronic quotation – 'death's effacing fingers' – though without noting that this was one of the earliest English poems to mention vampires.

Cesare Lombroso's theories about the 'criminal type'. Lombroso (1835–1909), an Italian doctor and criminologist, proposed the theory that criminals were actually biological throwbacks to an earlier stage of human mental development: they were atavistic.

Max Nordau's much-publicized (and, in the Nazi period, highly influential) theories about degeneration, outlined in a monograph published in 1892. Hence Van Helsing's diagnosis of Dracula in Chapter XXV:

> The Count is a criminal and of criminal type. Nordau and Lombroso would so classify him, and *qua* criminal he is of imperfectly formed mind . . .

REAL-LIFE INSPIRATIONS

Henry Irving (see above); Walt Whitman (see above); Henry Morton Stanley (the explorer); Franz Liszt (the composer); Richard Burton (see above); the Poet Laureate Alfred, Lord Tennyson; Jacques Damala (a Greek actor married to Sarah Bernhardt). All of these, at one time or another, have been proposed as the physical model for the Count. Some are quite plausible, others a little tenuous. One of Stoker's biographers, Barbara Belford, is convinced that Irving was the true original of the Count; and a number of critics have proposed that the novel is charged with Stoker's resentment at having allowed Irving to take over every aspect of his life with such intense, 'vampiric' force. One of the Penguin Classics editions of *Dracula* has a photograph on its cover of Irving as

Mephistopheles, from the Lyceum production of *Faust*.

It has also been suggested that the scene in which the undead Lucy Westrena is staked may have been influenced by the most macabre event in Victorian literary history: the exhumation of Elizabeth Siddal's body several years after her death. Elizabeth 'Lizzie' Siddal, widely agreed to be one of the most beautiful women of her age, was a muse figure to the men of the Pre-Raphaelite Brotherhood. She died in 1861, of a laudanum overdose; it may have been suicide, but she was permitted Christian burial in Highgate Cemetery. Distraught, her lover, the poet and painter Dante Gabriel Rossetti, placed in her coffin a notebook containing, among other things, the text of many unpublished poems.

Eight years later, Rossetti was in a bad way; he could not write, could not paint, and managed to convince himself he was going blind. In his frantic misery, he came up with the grisly idea of retrieving the notebook and somehow managed to secure legal permission for an exhumation. It took place at night, to keep the curious and ghoulish away; Rossetti was not present. When Siddal's coffin was opened, it was said that her body was hardly touched by decay, and her long red hair had grown longer in death so that it filled the coffin. The notebook, mildly worm-eaten, was plucked from her hair and she was reburied. Rossetti duly published the reclaimed poems, but guilt about his morbid initiative haunted him for the rest of his life.

WHO WAS THE REAL DRACULA?

Many reference books will simply tell you that Dracula is closely based on the fifteenth-century Wallachian Prince, or Warlord, who has long been known as Vlad Tepes, 'Vlad the Impaler' (c. 1430-1 to c. 1476), thanks to the legend that his favourite method of seeing off his enemies was to impale them on wooden stakes. It is reported that on one occasion, Vlad murdered some twenty thousand Turkish prisoners of war in this way, arranging their staked bodies in a giant semi-circle outside Wallachia's capital city, Tirgoviste, to frighten off other enemy troops. 'Dracula' means 'son of the Dragon'; Dracul – 'dragon' (though also, handily for Stoker's purposes, 'devil') – being the cognomen of Vlad the Impaler's father (c. 1390–1447).

The Romanian tourist industry is happy to perpetuate this identification – Wallachia is that part of contemporary Romania which lies south of the Transylvanian Alps – as are a few Dracula scholars. This habit of identifying the fictional Count with the real-life *Voivode*, or 'Prince', has become so widespread in the last few decades that, among vampire fans, 'Vlad' is now a readily understood nickname for the ancient fiend. There is some limited evidence for this understanding in the pages of Stoker's novel: Van Helsing says that Dracula ' . . . must, indeed, have been that Voivode Dracula who won his name against the Turk, over the great river on the very frontier of Turkey-land.' But it was not until the publication, in the early 1970s, of two best-selling books, *In Search of Dracula* by Raymond T. McNally and Radu Florescu (1972), and its sequel of the following year, *Dracula: A Biography of Vlad the Impaler, 1431–1476*, that the idea really took hold.

Film-makers picked up on the main thesis of these two historians almost immediately. The 1973 production of *Dracula*, by the producer/director Dan Curtis and the writer Richard Matheson, used the Vlad theory to supply their villain (played by Jack Palance) with a reason for being fascinated by Lucy Westenra – she looked identical to Vlad's beloved, who had died in the fifteenth century. James V. Hart, who wrote the screenplay for *Bram Stoker's Dracula* (1992), followed the same line, though in his script it is Mina Murray (apparently the reincarnation of Vlad's wife Elizabeth; Winona Ryder plays both parts) who obsesses the Count. More recently, Elizabeth Kostova's best-selling novel *The Historian* (2005) has also helped perpetuate the equation Drac = Vlad.

So: what is wrong with this theory?

Nothing much, except that it assumes both information and

intentions that Stoker never had. He had long since conceived the idea of his villain – 'Count Wampyr', as he named him at the time – when his assiduous researches turned up William Wilkinson's *Account of the Principalities of Wallachia and Moldavia* (1820), where he discovered the name 'Dracula' and liked the sound of it. 'Dracula in the Wallachian language means Devil,' Wilkinson notes. 'The Wallachians were, at that time, as they are at the present, used to give this as a surname to any person who rendered himself conspicuous either by courage, cruel actions, or cunning.' Vlad senior, Vlad Dracul, had been a member of the Order of the Dragon, a chivalric body dedicated, among other goals, to war against the armies of Islam. It was probably this allegiance that inspired his *nom de guerre*.

Before 1972, there had never been any recorded folkloric connection between the Voivode and vampirism. On the contrary, Vlad Tepes, for all his ruthlessness – he is estimated to have killed some forty thousand people in the course of his brief, six-year reign – was not a villain, but a national hero, admired for his gallant defence of the homeland against enemies, particularly the Turkish. He met his downfall in a campaign which began in 1461, and was planned to drive the Turkish forces from the Danube river valley south and west of Bucharest (a city he had built up from a small village; now capital of Romania). The tide of battle turned against him, and after a long retreat he escaped into Transylvania, where he was arrested by the Hungarian monarch Matthias Corvinus. He was eventually released, and in 1475 was once again recognized as Prince, but just a few months later he died at the hands of an assassin.

Vlad Tepes had a modest castle built for himself near the town of Poenari, overlooking the River Argefl in the foothill of the Transylvanian Alps. If there is a 'real' Castle Dracula, this is it. Stoker locates his vampire's castle as being near the Borgo Pass; he had never heard of Vlad's actual castle, and it seems fairly certain that his description of the Count's mountainous lair was drawn entirely from his imagination.

WHO WAS †HE REAL VAN HELSING?

Leaving aside the possibility that the Dutch savant was a pure invention, there are a couple of leading candidates for his original:

Arminius (or Armin) Vambery (1832–1913). A professor of Oriental languages at the University of Budapest (or Buda-Pesth, as was the standard spelling in Stoker's day), in his time a famous man of letters, and also a noted collector of fine wines. Stoker met him in 1890, in the very early days of work on his novel, at a dinner with Henry Irving and others at the Beefsteak Club. Stoker also paid an indirect compliment to Vambery by having Van Helsing refer to him in cordial terms ('I have asked my friend Arminius, of Buda-Pesth University, to make his record . . .').

Friedrich Max Müller (1823–1900). A professor of modern European languages and comparative philology at Oxford University. Christopher Frayling believes that Stoker and Müller were in correspondence at some time during the 1890s; and there is a surviving letter from Müller to Henry Irving, asking for a ticket to Faust, so it is quite possible that Stoker might have met the professor through his employer.

Stoker himself, in a spirit of idealized self-portraiture.

'Dr Martin Hasselius', the narrator of Sheridan Le Fanu's *In a Glass Darkly* (1872).

Sherlock Holmes. Fanciful readers have sometimes suggested that Van Helsing was actually Sherlock Holmes, in disguise. See page 77.

STOKER'S DRACULA LIBRARY

Stoker spent years researching texts that might be of use to him in composing his novel. Scholars have unearthed many of the books he definitely or probably consulted; here are a dozen from which he took detailed notes:

✝ Sabine Baring-Gould, *The Book of Were-Wolves: Being an Account of a Terrible Superstition* (1865).

✝ Isabella L. Bird, *The Golden Chersonese* (1883).

✝ Charles Boner, *Transylvania: Its Products and Its People* (1865).

✝ Sir Thomas Browne, *Religio Medici* (1643).

✝ Andrew F. Crosse, *Round About the Carpathians* (1878).

✝ A Fellow of the Carpathian Society, *Magyarland: Being the Narrative of our Travels through the Highlands and Lowlands of Hungary* (1881).

✝ Emily Gerard, *The Land Beyond the Forest* (1885, especially the chapter 'Transylvanian Superstitions').

✝ Major E. C. Johnson, *On the Track of the Crescent: Erratic Notes from the Piraeus to Pesth* (1885).

✝ F. C. and J. Rivington, *The Theory of Dreams* (1808).

✝ F. K. Robinson, *A Whitby Glossary* (1876).

✝ Robert H. Scott, *Fishery Barometer Manual* (1887).

✝ William Wilkinson, *An Account of the Principalities of Wallachia and Moldavia; with various Political Observations Relating to Them* (1820).

WHAT DOES 'NOSFERATU' MEAN?

Van Helsing seems to think it means 'vampire'.

Stoker found the word in Emily Gerard's *The Land Beyond the Forest* (1885): 'More decidedly evil is the *nosferatu*, or vampire, in which every Roumanian peasant believes as he does in heaven or hell.' Van Helsing follows her use of the word: 'The *nosferatu* do not die like the bee when he stings once. He is only stronger, and being stronger, have yet more power to work evil.'

But some commentators have questioned Gerard's accuracy, since the word is not known in modern Romanian, and does not even appear to be a known dialect term. Either, they conclude, she made it up, or she mangled the transcription of some other word, possibly *nesuferit* – 'not to be suffered', 'intolerable'.

The vampire encyclopedist J. Gordon Melton suggests that the word, though unrecorded in dictionaries, nonetheless existed for centuries in common speech, carried over from the Old Slavonic term *nesufer-atu*, itself derived from the Greek *nosphoros*: 'plague carrier'. The term became well known in English – though you will still not find it in the *Oxford English Dictionary* – after the international success of Murnau's 1922 film *Nosferatu*.

DRACULA AND SHERLOCK HOLMES

Rubbish, Watson, rubbish! What have we to do with walking corpses who can only be held in their graves by stakes driven through their hearts? It's pure lunacy.

'The Adventure of the Sussex Vampire' (1924)

No other fictional characters have been so frequently the subject of films, dramas, novels, comics and parodies as these two products of the late Victorian period. (Holmes first made his appearance in 1887, ten years before *Dracula*, in the pages of *Beeton's Christmas Annual*.) *Dracula* is reckoned by some sources to be the novel most frequently raided for films (there are now more than 150 films in which Dracula is a main character, and countless other apparently Count-less films in which he – or some thinly veiled equivalent – plays a significant role), though others insist that it is Holmes who takes the lead with over 200 movie adaptations to his credit. Most readers will be content to assume that the master vampire and the great detective are probably pretty much neck and (bitten) neck.

In an age of pastiche and homage, it was almost inevitable that the two characters should one day meet, especially after the novelist and director Nicholas Meyer introduced Bram Stoker as a character in his Holmesian fiction *The West End Horror* (1976). Subsequent arenas in which the two Victorians have clashed include:

Sherlock Holmes vs. Dracula: The Adventures of the Sanguinary Count by Loren D. Estleman (1979; though attributed to 'Dr John H. Watson'). Holmes is called in to investigate the wreck of the Demeter, then picks up on newspaper reports of the 'Bloofer Lady' stalking Hampstead Heath.

The Holmes-Dracula File by Fred Saberhagen (1978). This is one of a series of novels in which Dracula is portrayed as gravely misunderstood, and the real villain of the story is Dr Seward.

Scarlet in Gaslight by Martin Powell (1987). A four-part comic published to mark the centenary of Holmes's debut. It includes a dastardly plan by Professor Moriarty to unleash a plague of vampires on London. For their own reasons, Holmes and Dracula eventually team up, and Dracula kills Moriarty – for the second time, as it were – at the Reichenbach Falls.

The Tangled Skein by David Stuart Davies (1995). A variant on *The Hound of the Baskervilles*.

The greatest of all the actors to have played Holmes, Jeremy Brett, also took the part of Dracula for the Broadway production of the late 1970s. Oh, to have seen it.

COUNT DOWN: TWENTY-FIVE ACTORS WHO HAVE PLAYED DRACULA

† Bela Lugosi (in the 1931 Tod Browning film and others).

✝ Lon Chaney Jr (in *Son of Dracula*).

✝ John Carradine (in *House of Frankenstein* and many, many others).

✝ Christopher Lee (in the Hammer series and other productions).

✝ Denholm Elliott (in the Thames Television production, 1968).

✝ Jack Palance (in the 1973 film).

✝ Udo Kier (in *Blood for Dracula* and others).

✝ David Niven (in *Old Dracula*).

✝ Frank Langella (on Broadway and in the John Badham film).

✝ Jeremy Brett (on Broadway).

✝ Raul Julia (on Broadway).

✝ John Le Clerc (on Broadway).

✝ David Dukes (on Broadway).

✝ Terence Stamp (in the London production of the Broadway show).

✝ Louis Jourdan (in the BBC mini-series, 1978).

✝ Gary Oldman (in *Bram Stoker's Dracula*).

✝ Leslie Nielsen (in *Dracula: Dead and Loving It*).

✝ George Hamilton (in *Love at First Bite*).

✝ Gerald Butler (in *Dracula 2001*).

✝ Patrick Bergin (in an Italian production, 2002).

✝ Dominic Purcell ('Drake' in *Blade: Trinity*).

✝ Richard Roxburgh (in *Van Helsing*).

✝ Rudolph Martin (in *Buffy the Vampire Slayer*, 26 September 2000).

✝ Marc Warren (in the 2006 BBC Production).

✝ Bruno Pelletier (in a 2006 musical version).

But there have been literally hundreds of others. The Internet Movie Database (IMDb) lists more than two hundred actors who have played the part or some close variant in cinema and television films.

DRACULA's England

In or near London:

'Carfax' at Purfleet. The estate bought by Count Dracula; immediately next door to the private lunatic asylum run by Dr Seward. 'Carfax' is Stoker's invention.

London Zoo. From which the 'Berserker' wolf escapes.

Hampstead Heath. Where the undead Lucy Westenra stalks human prey as the 'Bloofer Lady'. (The Westenra family is said to live in 'Hillingham', which is probably Hampstead.)

Highgate Cemetery. The most likely location of Lucy's tomb - there are some ambiguities.

The Lyceum Theatre. Stoker worked here during the years he was researching and writing his novel.

The East End. Dracula hides many of his specially prepared coffins at various sites around the district, including Mile End and Bermondsey.

Piccadilly. Holmwood stays here, at the Albemarle Hotel; so, too, does Van Helsing, at the Berkeley (now moved to Knightsbridge); Harker drinks tea at the A.B.C. at number 27; and Dracula rents a house here for his central London base, at number 347. (An imaginary number, though the property described by Stoker is like an amalgam of numbers 138 and 139.)

Outside London:

Bray Studios. Location for the filming of the Hammer 'Dracula' series.

Exeter. Where Jonathan Harker is employed as a solicitor by Mr Peter Hawkins.

Whitby. Where Lucy and Mina spend a fateful holiday; and where the 'Demeter' is wrecked. It is home to a minor tourist attraction called the Dracula Experience.

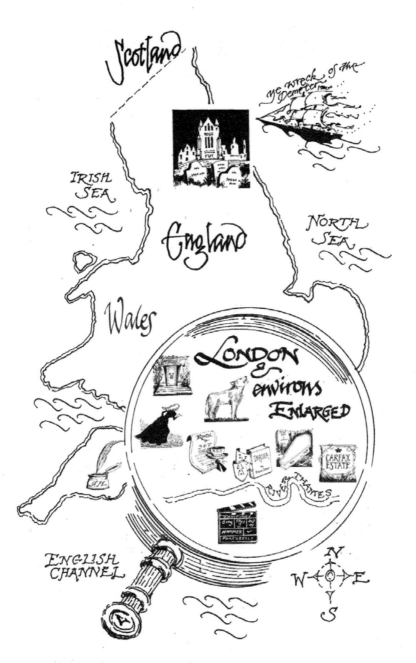

Scotland

ye wreck of the Demeter

IRISH SEA

England

NORTH SEA

Wales

LONDON & environs ENLARGED

CARFAX ESTATE

RIVER THAMES

HAMMER PINEWOOD

ENGLISH CHANNEL

N W E S

FOUR

PRINTS OF DARKNESS,
c.1920 to c.1980

THE TWENTIETH-CENTURY VAMPIRE,
FROM MURNAU TO HERZOG
*In which, among other triumphs, vampires invade
the new technology of cinema . . .*

EARLY SIGHTINGS

It has been suggested that the very first glimpse of vampires on the big screen came merely months after the birth of cinema, in a two-minute film by Méliès, *Le Manoir du diable* (1896), which shows a bat metamorphosing into a demon figure. In fact, there are any number of early films with 'vampire' or 'vamp' in the title, but most of these simply follow in the vein of the Philip Burne-Jones painting, and are about seductive women. Louis Feuillade's series *Les Vampires* (1915) is misleading in a different way, since his supposedly undead villains prove to be human, and an ingenious gang of super-thieves. *Les Vampires* starred an actress known as 'Musidora', sporting a slinky black jumpsuit, as 'Irma Vep' – yes, an anagram of 'vampire'. The series was a great favourite of the Surrealists; and the French director Olivier Assayas paid homage to it a few years ago in his film *Irma Vep* (1996).

In Hollywood, there were at least two authentically Gothic shorts: *The Vampire* (1913) and *The Village Vampire* (1916). There is some evidence that a vampire film was produced in the latter days of Imperial Russia, entitled *The Secret of House No. 5* (1912). The Soviet Union supposedly produced a *Dracula* – a Marxist parable? – circa 1920, though no prints survive. And there was a Hungarian production, *Drakula*, in 1921. But it was not until 1922 that the fledgling bat-creature took flight.

THE HAUNTED SCREEN

Nosferatu, eine Symphonie des Grauens

So *Nosferatu* (1922, directed by F. W. Murnau) is not literally the very first vampire film. It is certainly the first, though, to be directed by an indisputable giant of the cinema: F. W. Murnau. (If you don't have undue reverence for, say, Coppola, Polanski or Herzog, you might say that it remains the only one. Ingmar Bergman is said to have been interested in making a Dracula film, but nothing came of it. And see the section on Orson Welles, below.) It is still one of the greatest of all vampire movies.

The film was a loose adaptation of the Stoker novel, though not so loose as to escape the jealous attentions and litigation of the author's widow, Florence. The man who dreamed up the film was a strange character by the name of Albin Grau, an architect and painter who was obsessed by spiritualism and other aspects of the occult. Though Murnau usually reaps artistic credit for its supernatural beauty, it may well be that Grau was the true author. Grau's esoteric tastes can be deduced from the name of *Nosferatu*'s production company, Prana-Film, *prana* being a Buddhist concept meaning, roughly, the breath of life. Some of the eerily convincing aspects of the film may be attributed to the fact that Grau actually believed in vampires – or, at least, claimed that he did.

In an article published in 1921, while *Nosferatu* was in pre-production, Grau told the yarn of something that had happened to him and his army comrades while on an inglorious delousing assignment in Serbia, some time in 1916 – the point of the exercise being to fend off a potential epidemic of typhus. (An interesting note, in view of the threat, and metaphor, of plague in the completed film.) The job was simple if unpleasant, and consisted mainly of forcibly shaving the heads of unwilling villagers. At night, as the snowstorm blew around their ill-heated billet, the talk turned to the supernatural.

At this moment, an old peasant came forward and, making the sign of the cross, told the men that he had seen a vampire in Romania, 'an undead or a Nosferatu, as vampires are called over there,' and explained that his father had been killed by a falling tree-trunk and then buried without the sacred rites. Four weeks later, locals began to spread the terrifying rumour that the dead man had returned, and was raiding houses at night, killing the tenants. Eventually, a brave posse went to the man's grave one night, opened it up, and found it empty. The next day (18 May 1884, according to an official form the peasant waved at Grau and his team by way of proof), the men returned, found the vampire and staked it in the approved manner. The old man's tale, Grau said, had haunted him ever since.

Whatever the truth of this anecdote, Grau recognized *Dracula* as a suitable subject for the cinema, and commissioned an industry veteran, Henrik Galeen, as the screenwriter. As director, he chose a former protégé of Max Reinhardt, F. W. Murnau. They set to work. Among the strategic changes made by the team to Stoker's outline were:

✝ Changing the setting of the second half from London in the 1890s to Germany (mainly Bremen) in the 1830s.

✝ Renaming principal characters: Count Dracula becomes Graf Orlok, Jonathan Harker becomes Waldemar Hutter, Mina Murray – here the hero's wife rather than his fiancée – becomes Ellen Hutter; Renfield becomes Knock; and Van Helsing becomes Bulwar.

✝ Radically altering the vampire's appearance. The actor Max Shreck (whose surname means 'terror') is an unnerving sight even to today's relatively hard-bitten viewers: painfully thin, bald, with long, claw-like nails. Rather than the conventional over-developed canines, his fangs are set at the front of his mouth, underlining his similarity to the plague rats he brings in his wake. (Rats, rather than bats, are the vampiric totem animal in *Nosferatu*.)

✝ Introducing the potent idea that Orlok's arrival in Bremen – accompanied by a gigantic swarm of rats – is the coming of a plague.

✝ Having the vampire cast shadows (to considerable dramatic effect).

Otherwise the story runs recognizably along the same lines as Stoker's, until the film's dramatic conclusion when Orlok is tricked by the noble Frau Hutter, at the expense of her own life, into exposing himself to daylight, which makes him vanish in a mildly bathetic puff of smoke – thus creating a key vampire myth which persists in virtually all of today's productions (or which has to be carefully explained away in expository dialogue as 'myth').

Nosferatu was shot in the summer of 1921, mostly on location – an unusual practice at the time, adopted because it was cheaper than building sets, though it also had the advantage of filling Murnau's work with real scenery. Critics have compared its vistas of nature with those of great landscape painters such as Caspar David Friedrich. Night scenes were shot in the daylight, and tinted later to give the impression of gloom.

It premiered in March 1922 at the Berlin Zoological Gardens, where the screening was accompanied by an orchestra, playing an original score from the composer Hans Erdmann.

Within a matter of weeks, Florence Stoker had contacted the Society of Authors to intervene on her behalf, and battle was on. Prana-Film fell into financial chaos and went out of business; all of its planned films were abandoned. In 1925, German courts ruled in Mrs

Stoker's favour, and ordered all prints destroyed. Fortunately, a few escaped. One of the pirated prints eventually reached New York in 1929, where it was screened at the avant-garde Film Guild Cinema in Greenwich Village . . . to anti-climactic effect. Reviews were mostly lukewarm, at best, and in the wake of this indifference, the film itself remained largely forgotten until the 1960s and 1970s, when, as part of a gathering wave of interest in silent film generally and Weimar cinema in particular, film scholars began to recover prints from various archives, including Langlois's Cinémathèque Français. Neglect gave way to admiration, and canonization; *Nosferatu* has been called 'perhaps the greatest of Weimar films' (Gilberto Perez).

Who Was F. W. Murnau?

Murnau has been called 'the German cinema's most exquisite Romantic poet'.

Born in 1888, the son of a textile manufacturer, Friedrich Wilhelm Plumpe adopted the surname 'Murnau' as a young man, partly as an act of homage to the artists' colony of that name south of Munich, visited by the likes of Kandinsky and Franz Marc. From 1911 to 1914, he lived in Berlin as a pupil of Max Reinhardt at the Deutsche Schauspielhaus, where he worked both as an actor and as an assistant director. In 1915, Murnau was called up by the infantry and posted to East Prussia. Desperately bored, he transferred to the Luftwaffe in 1916 and flew a number of missions over France until an emergency landing during fog left him trapped in Switzerland for the rest of the war.

After demobilization, Murnau returned to Germany and soon found employment in the film industry. His earliest efforts established his affinity with supernatural themes: *Der Januskopf* (1920), a loose adaptation of the Jekyll and Hyde theme (incidentally featuring both Bela Lugosi and a major actor of the Weimar period, Conrad Veidt), and *The Haunted Castle* (1921). After *Nosferatu*, Murnau was given a great deal of artistic licence, and made two of the other great German classics of the time, *The Last Laugh* (1924) and *Faust* (1926). As was common at the time, he was soon poached by Hollywood, and there made *Sunrise* (1927), today regarded as a high-water mark of the silent cinema (indeed, of all cinema). After a strange and ill-conceived collaboration with Robert Flaherty which resulted in his last completed work, *Tabu*, he died in a car crash in 1931.

Nosferatu's Legacy

Murnau's film, in the spirit of Graf Orlok, has cast a very long shadow. It continues to be screened and enjoyed in its own right (there is now a very handsome double-disc DVD), and for the works it has influenced or inspired – above all, the 1979 remake by Werner Herzog. Barlow, the chief vampire in Tobe Hooper's television film of *Salem's Lot* (1979), is a ringer for Count Orlok, and the vampires in *30 Days of Night* (1997), though not identical in looks, deliberately reprise the *Nosferatu* motif of the undead as hideous fanged predators.

There have also been a number of fictions about Murnau and his film, of which the best-known is *Shadow of the Vampire*, starring John Malkovich as the director. Its main conceit is that Max Shreck – wonderfully played by Willem Dafoe – was an actual vampire, tracked down by Murnau in his craze for authenticity; so that the film is a sort of Faustian parable about the ruthlessness of the obsessed artist. There has also been a short novel, *Nosferatu in Love*, by Jim Shepard, which concentrates on the gay aspect of Murnau's life. Finally, it would be criminal not to mention that running gag on the BBC comedy series *The Fast Show*, in which the protean Paul Whitehouse, made up as Count Orlok, creeps into a maiden's bed-chamber at night . . . and gives her racing tips.

THE LOST 'VAMPIRE' FILM

Hollywood's first full-scale 'vampire' film, *London After Midnight* (1927) was directed by Tod Browning (who went on to direct the 1931 *Dracula* starring Bela Lugosi), and starred Lon Chaney Sr in two roles – a Scotland yard detective, and a wild-eyed 'vampire'; the reason for the inverted commas is that he turns out not to be a real vampire after all, but the detective himself working undercover, with an elaborate make-up job. Stills of Chaney bugging his eyes at the camera are often reproduced in histories of the early cinema, but the negative and all the known prints of this film have long since disappeared. (Rumours that it has finally been discovered persist to an annoying degree.) Browning had the chance to remake the film as a talkie in 1935 as *Mark of the Vampire*, this time with Bela Lugosi in the role of 'Count Mora' and Lionel Atwill as the detective.

THE ELUSIVE DANISH VAMPIRE

There are those who hold that the greatest vampire film ever made was the work of the Danish director, Carl Theodor Dreyer: *Vampyr* (1932); also known as *The Strange Adventures of David Gray* (UK) and *The Vampire or Castle of Doom* (USA). I do not for a second dispute its greatness – it is profoundly strange and disconcerting, and when I first saw it, its ghostly play with shadows and the fragile condition of sanity troubled my sleep for a couple of nights – but will not discuss it at length here because, even though it is notionally based on Le Fanu's *Carmilla*, the vampiric content of the work is slight to the point of being well-nigh invisible. The vampire of the film takes the form of an aged crone; she scarcely appears.

Dreyer's film is the subject of an impassioned BFI (British Film Institute) monograph by the English playwright David Rudkin; highly recommended.

DRACULA GOES TO HOLLYWOOD

Stage Blood II: *Dracula, the Vampire Play*

The first stage adaptation of Stoker's novel since the author's own marathon version of 1897 was made by an Anglo-Irish actor who had met Stoker in 1889, when employed by the Henry Irving Vacation Company: Hamilton Deane. Deane had been trying in vain to find an established dramatist willing to write the adaptation, and in the end wrote the play himself while confined to bed with a cold. Florence Stoker agreed to sell Deane the dramatic rights to the novel, though she was never entirely happy with the way it turned out.

Dracula, the Vampire Play (the full title; hereafter, just *Dracula*) was licensed by the Lord Chamberlain on 5 August 1924, and had a trial run at the Grand Theatre, Derby. Deane took the part of Abraham Van Helsing; Dracula was played by Edmund Blake. Deane's work was well received, and the following year he moved it south, to a small theatre in Wimbledon. Finally, on 14 February 1927, *Dracula* received its West End premiere at the Little Theatre. The reviews were derisive, but the public ignored what the critics wrote and came in their hordes. The box office remained brisk, and the play transferred to the Duke of York's Theatre that summer; eventually, it took up residence at the Prince of Wales Theatre.

An American entrepreneur, Horace Liveright, had been watching these developments carefully . . .

He approached the American journalist and playwright John L. Balderston to adapt the play for its New York premiere, and the resulting work became the version which left its mark on the 1931 film of *Dracula* – and, thus, on the world. Two of the original cast, Richard Huntley and Bernard Jukes, were offered the chance to play their London roles of Dracula and Renfield, but only Jukes accepted;

and so the part was offered to Bela Lugosi, a forty-six-year-old Hungarian émigré who had arrived in New York in 1920, but still had very poor English; he learned his roles phonetically, which lent a certain eccentric charm to his line readings.

After a try-out at the Schubert Theater, New Haven, the American version opened at the Fulton Theater in New York on 5 October 1927. The reviews were much better than those for the London production, and the show was soon established as a hit; it ran for thirty-three weeks before audiences began to fall off, and then went on tour to the West Coast. Again, it was a smash hit, and further tours in the Midwest and elsewhere established *Dracula* as a national craze. By the end of its run, the production had earned Liveright almost $2 million.

Inevitably, Hollywood took note.

What the Playwrights Did

The Deane and Balderston *Dracula* compresses the events of Stoker's novel into three acts – and a very, very short epilogue. (I base this account on the text published by Samuel French, Inc., in 1927.)

ONE: The library of Dr Seward's sanatorium, Purley. Evening.
TWO: Lucy's boudoir. Evening of the following day.
THREE: Scene I. The same as Act One. Thirty-two hours later. (Shortly before sunrise.)
Scene II: A vault. Just after sunrise.
Epilogue: Spoken to AUDIENCE by Van Helsing.

In other words, Deane and Balderston threw out all of the Translyvanian business, and reduced the characters to a cast of eight, including a comic asylum attendant and a maid. They saw off Mina Harker, who has died (of vampire bites; it is she rather than Lucy who becomes the 'Bloofer Lady', whose predations are reported but not dramatized) just before the action begins. Dr Seward, now middle-aged, is Lucy's father rather than her suitor. Lucy is suffering from a dangerously severe loss of blood; Count Dracula, a new neighbour, appears entirely charming and even offers her his blood for a transfusion. The rest is reasonably familiar, with one or two nice twists: Dracula, we learn, has come to England – via Croydon Aerodrome – by plane: 'Five centuries pass. The aeroplane is invented. His chance has come, for now he can cross Europe in a single night . . .'

It's not much better than workmanlike, but it helped make the 1931 movie what it is.

Bela Figura: the Browning Version

The Universal film of *Dracula*, directed by Tod Browning and released in February 1931, finally made the Count a brand name familiar around the world. It was also the only profitable film the Universal studios made that year, and helped rescue Universal from the Depression. (At the end of 2008, as the stock markets tumbled and the *Twilight* books did a roaring trade, some cultural historians began to muse on the link between depressions and vampires.) And by showing that there was a vast, in fact virtually limitless, appetite for supernatural and horrific themes, it is largely responsible for launching the horror film genre as we know it today.

So it is quite surprising to watch the film again today, and notice with mounting boredom how ropey most of it is.

Almost everything about it which is still worth watching comes in the opening Transylvanian section. In contrast to Stoker's novel, it is Renfield (Dwight Frye, epicene and eerie in the film's other memorable performance, alongside Lugosi's), not Harker, who travels to Dracula's castle, by way of all the usual dark peasant mutterings, proffering of crucifixes and so on. Dracula's castle is a thing of magnificent decay, draped in cobwebs so thick that Renfield has to thrash them away with his walking stick, and swarming with all sort of creatures of ill omen: spiders, rats . . . and, in defiance of zoological orthodoxy, armadillos. Much of the film is conducted in silence – remember that the talkies were barely three years old – and the lack of soundtrack is doubtless a lot more unnerving to us than it was to its original audience.

What little dialogue there is has passed into folklore: 'Listen to them, children of the night – what music they make!'; 'I do not drink . . . wine.'; 'The blood is the life, Mr Renfield.' Lugosi speaks these lines in a heavily accented English with unexpected stress patterns; no wonder, as he was still learning his parts by ear. But he manages the necessary transitions from suave and ingratiating to murderous with great aplomb, aided by what is technically known as a 'kick' light, which isolates his mad, staring eyes and makes them glow against the surrounding gloom. He might not be a masterful actor, but he is an unforgettable presence.

After the Stoker-inspired scene in which three female vampires move in to attack Renfield and are made to back down – again, all this is shot in unnerving silence – we cut to not very convincing footage of a ship on the high seas, fighting a storm (here, it is called the *Vesta*, not the *Demeter*), and to the newly insane Renfield lurking and plotting in its hold with his master. The film's last farewell to imaginative shooting style comes when the ship docks: we see only the shadow of the dead captain, lashed to his wheel, as unseen cockney voices talk about this unaccountable tragedy. From this point on, it is as if Browning lost all interest in the film. In fact, there are rumours that the cinematographer, Karl Freund, had to take over a lot of the directing chores, which may explain why he had no energy left to exercise his considerable talents as a director of photography.

All of Dracula's exploits in modern-day London, from his first appearance murdering a flower-girl to his last-reel staking – off-screen! – by Van Helsing, are shot flatly and unimaginatively, and for the most part with a static camera. There isn't much attempt to disguise the theatrical origins of these scenes, and where the overture was imposingly silent, the body of the film is much too talky; not very well-crafted talk, at that. The film teems with lazy howlers, such as locating Whitby in the suburbs of London (a gaffe carried over into *Dracula's Daughter*).

In short, the Browning *Dracula* is a botched job, barely worth viewing after the first twenty minutes or so. So why did it have such a shattering impact? Partly because audiences had never seen the like before, and loved the unfamiliar frisson it gave them; partly because Lugosi's screen presence is remarkably powerful, and no less so for being wrapped in plenty of first-grade ham. And, most of all, partly because of Stoker's talent as a maker of myths.

Who Was Tod Browning?

Tod Browning (1882–1962) is one of the most intriguing figures in the early history of Hollywood: often a recluse, unfortunately an alcoholic, and always an enigma. He made plenty of money at his trade, and retired, comfortably off, at the end of the 1930s, but has generally been neglected by critics and historians until quite recently. Of his many other movies, the only one to have earned much critical attention is the extraordinary and much-banned *Freaks* (1933) – a feature film acted largely by real-life performers in a travelling show. (Browning had been a carny performer in his early years, before taking work as a screen actor.) Sometimes derided for his sloppiness, he nonetheless deserves credit for having so satisfactorily 'opened out' the stage play with the Castle Dracula scenes – the scenes by which the film is best remembered.

Who Was Bela Lugosi?

Born Bela Blasko on 20 October 1882 in Lugos, Hungary, he began his stage career proper in 1902, adopting the stage name Lugosi – 'from

Lugos'. He moved to Germany after the war and, in 1920, to America, where he was granted political asylum. He managed to find acting work despite his poor English, and had his big break with the stage version of *Dracula* in 1927. Universal wanted Lon Chaney Sr to play the role on screen, but Chaney died, thus giving Lugosi his big break. *Dracula* made him a star almost immediately and brought him a huge fan base of adoring women.

After *Dracula*, most of his screen appearances were in horror movies or thrillers: *Murders in the Rue Morgue*, *White Zombie*. He never played Dracula again on screen – apart from his cameo in an Abbott and Costello comedy – though he frequently revived the part on stage, both in America and in England. He was briefly cast as Frankenstein's monster for the Universal production, but the role went to Boris Karloff. He worked hard, at one time completing as many as five films a year; steering very close to the copyright wind, he appeared as the Dracula-like figure 'Armand Tesla' in the Columbia production *Return of the Vampire* (1943). His career went into a bad decline by the end of the forties, when the horror cycle ran down. At one point, stuck in England and penniless at the end of one of his theatrical tours, he agreed to play another Dracula-like character in a pitifully poor British comedy, *Old Mother Riley Meets the Vampire*. (Lugosi's character, wearing full evening dress, is in fact a mad scientist, who has created a killer robot.) He became addicted to painkilling drugs and, notoriously, played his final role in 'the worst film ever made' – Ed Wood's *Plan 9 from Outer Space* – dying before the film was complete on 16 August 1956. He was buried in his Dracula cloak.

LOS HIJOS DE LA NOCHE: THE SPANISH DRÁCULA

Forgotten for many years in the English-speaking world, this very unusual production by George Melford (1931) was restored to public awareness by the film scholar David J. Skal in his splendidly researched and highly readable book *Hollywood Gothic*. Intended for sale south of the border, the film was made with an entirely hispanophone cast. It was shot over the course of just twenty-two nights on the very same sets used by Browning and company during the day. Browning would wrap at six, and the cast and crew of the Spanish *Drácula* would simply take their places. Carlos Villarias, a stage actor from Córdoba, was cast in the Lugosi role; Lupita Tovar, a seventeen-year-old Mexican, was cast as 'Eva', the Mina character; Carmen Guerrero as 'Lucia'; Eduardo Arozamena as Van Helsing; and a multilingual actor (purportedly from Argentina), Barry Norton, as 'Juan Harker'.

The director was the American George Melford, who spoke no Spanish, and relied on a translator, E. Tovar Avalos; the excellent cinematographer was George Robinson. Together, they brought to the shooting script a fluency of camera movement, a felicity of composition and a creative use of shadows that – combined with sexier, more full-blooded performances by the cast – have left most watchers persuaded that this is a far better film than Browning's. It is now quite easily available on DVD.

CITIZEN FANG: ORSON WELLES'S DRACULA

In conversation with Peter Bogdanovich, Welles once puckishly observed that *Dracula* was a very good story, and that 'someone should really make a film out of it . . .' What he meant, of course, was that none of the movie versions to date had drawn directly from Stoker's novel (and, with the exception of the 1977 BBC version, this remains the case. For the case of *Bram Stoker's Dracula*, see Chapter Five). If only someone had given Welles the backing to make that film . . .

We do, though, have some indication as to what Welles might have made of it. He staged *Dracula* on the radio, using his fast-moving adaptation of Stoker's book to launch his *Mercury Theatre on the Air* series on CBS radio in 1938. Boiled down to less than an hour (to allow room for CBS announcements and one commercial break), the Welles *Dracula* does adhere to the general outlines of Stoker's novel, and in particular makes quite a meal of the final chase back to Transylvania. The action is narrated by Dr Seward, here young again and engaged to Lucy; Welles plays both Seward and – in a deep, booming voice – the Count, who does not have many lines, most of those he does have being variants on, 'Flesh of my Flesh . . . Blood of my Blood.'

It is slightly hokey at times, particularly when it resorts to blaring orchestral chords to beef up the shock value – Bernard Hermann provided the musical score – but the acting is fine, and the action, heavily spiced with sound effects (railway whistles, galloping hooves, church bells, howling wolves), moves at a headlong pace. An interesting final touch: Mina, having apparently succumbed entirely to Dracula's mind control, snaps out of her trance at the very last possible second, and stakes Dracula herself. And once the play is done, Welles – borrowing from the stage play – comes on and, after some mock-soothing gags, declares that 'such things do exist'.

Welles fans should not miss Kim Newman's story in the *Anno Dracula* series, 'The Other Side of Midnight', in which Orson finally has the chance to make his vampire film; see Chapter Five.

BLOOD RUNS THIN: THE UNIVERSAL DRACULA SERIES

Despite the great success of their horror films, Universal only made a few more vampire films, and often rather mongrel, half-hearted or frankly silly ones at that: *Dracula's Daughter* (1936), *Son of Dracula* (1943), *House of Frankenstein* (1944), *House of Dracula* (1945) and *Abbott and Costello Meet Frankenstein* (1948) – the title of this last production being itself a fairly good indication of how the franchise was dying inch by inch. The last few need not detain us long, but the first two are not without merit.

Dracula's Daughter (1936, directed by Lambert Hillyer from a screenplay by Garret Fort, who also adapted the stage play for Tod Browning). This sequel is often said to have been inspired by Stoker's short story 'Dracula's Guest', though the resemblance is hard to find, save for the presence in both works of a female vampire. Edward Van Sloan reprises his 1931 role as Van Helsing, and the film picks up where Browning left off, at Carfax Abbey, where the police discover him with the corpses of Renfield and – staked – Dracula himself. Reasonably enough, the police arrest Van Helsing for murder, judging that his claim that the latter corpse is more than five hundred years old might not stand up in court. Van Helsing is jailed at 'Whitby'; once again, this is not on the Yorkshire coast but in a suburb of London.

Enter the star: Gloria Holden as the Countess Marya Zaleska, of Hungary. She rescues her father's remains, and with the help of her sinister henchman Sandor, burns them, in a rite designed to free her from the curse of vampirism that would otherwise be her inheritance. (An early example of the theme of vampirism-as-curse that would later become commonplace in the cinema.) She returns to her rented rooms above a bookshop in London, and tries to live a normal, human life. In vain. Meanwhile, Van Helsing is still trying to escape prison, and calls in help from his former pupil Dr Jeffrey Garth, and Garth's cute assistant Janet Blake. (All the other characters from *Dracula* have disappeared, without comment.)

Enter a lesbian subtext – not so very sub, really. The Countess sets herself up as an artist, and has Sandor recruit a frail young woman (Nan Grey, as Lili) to 'model' for her . . . and be her supper. The girl just about survives these attentions, at least long enough to be an informer to Garth. The London police, now suddenly firm believers in vampirism, conclude that Dracula is back and on the prowl, though Van Helsing insists that some new undead creature or creatures must be at work. The Countess – by now rather smitten with Garth – kidnaps Janet and flees to Transylvania. After the usual dark mutterings of peasants at the Borgo Pass, Garth makes it to Castle Dracula in time for the climax. Sandor, jealous of the Countess's plan to make Garth immortal like her, lets fly with an arrow, possibly meaning to kill his rival, but actually killing his mistress. Van Helsing and the bobbies arrive on the scene just in time to gun down Sandor.

Son of Dracula (1943, directed by Robert Siodmak, from a screenplay by Curt Siodmak). This is a very long way from being a true sequel, and it makes no reference at all to the events of the first two films. Its title is also odd, for the 'Son' (Lon Chaney Jr) seems to be none other than Dracula himself, hiding under the contemptibly flimsy alias of 'Count Alucard' – the first of countless occasions on which that reversal stunt has been used: see *Dracula A.D. 1972*, *Batman vs. Dracula* . . . (If this middle-aged fellow is indeed the 'son' of the Lugosi Dracula we have seen destroyed, nothing in the movie explains the blood relation.) But it's not a bad effort: Chaney, if a bit on the tubby side, is a haughty Dracula, and the well-shot swamp scenes – it is set in the deep South, presumably Louisiana – bear the authentic whiff of Southern Gothic.

The plot is moderately complex, but, briefly: Count Alucard/Dracula has travelled to modern-day America, in search of the blood of 'a young and vital race', and at the invitation of Katherine 'Kay' Caldwell, a rather morbid young woman fascinated by the occult. He arrives by train, in a crate containing his coffin. On the very night of Dracula's arrival, Kay's father, Colonel Caldwell, unexpectedly dies, as does a strange old gypsy woman, Kay's tutor in the secret arts. The Colonel bequeaths the estate, Dark Oaks, to Kay and leaves all his money to her sister, Claire. Kay suddenly and inexplicably jilts her long-term lover, Frank, and announces her marriage to the Count. Dr Brewster, an old family friend, is deeply suspicious, and calls in the help of a Hungarian savant, Professor Laszlo (the movie's Van Helsing figure), who 'solves' the Alucard/Dracula business.

Frank, mad with jealousy, makes his way into Dark Oaks and shoots at Alucard . . . but the bullets appear to pass through him harmlessly, and accidentally kill Kay instead. Or do they? Frank flees through the swamp, pursued by Alucard in the form of a bat (this was also the first film to include a full-blown special-effect transformation of Dracula to bat; Browning had relied on cuts), and takes refuge with Brewster. The doctor resolves to investigate, but when he goes to Dark Oaks, he finds to his bewilderment that Kay is still alive. The weird couple send him away, explaining coolly that they will be conducting scientific experiments that will leave them no time for social life.

Frank turns himself over to the sheriff, confessing to murder. The police accompany him and Brewster to Dark Oaks, where they find Kay's dead body in a coffin. Frank is arrested, and the body transferred to the morgue. But the undead Kay manifests herself to Frank in the form of a mist, explains that she wants to share her gift of immortal life with him, and springs him from jail with instructions as to how to kill Dracula. Frank sets off, the police not far behind, and finds Dracula's coffin. Dracula counter-attacks, but too late: the sunlight destroys him. A happy ending? Not quite. Frank realizes that Kay is doomed to vampiric existence forever, so he sets fire to her . . .

The last three Universal films can be dispatched briefly. *House of Frankenstein* (1944), also scripted by Curt Siodmak, features John Carradine as Count Dracula. (Carradine went on to play the role in many a dreadful production, including the next film in the sequence, *House of Dracula*, and the notoriously shoddy 1966 film *Billy the Kid vs. Dracula*.) It is a showcase for all three of Universal's big box-office monsters – Dracula, the Frankenstein creature, and the Wolf Man – and the vampiric sequence is over in less than half an hour. In this film, Dracula – whose remains are being exhibited in a travelling raree show – is brought back to life in full evening dress by having the stake removed from his rib cage. He is seen off, after various alarms and excursions, by daylight.

In *House of Dracula* (1945), the Count is once again back from the dead, with no explanation. He arrives at the very start of the film in the form of a bat, then reverts to humanoid form to confront Dr Edlemann, a scientist. Dracula is, he tells the doctor, craving to find a medical cure for his condition. (This notion that vampirism might be a biological rather than a supernatural state has become commonplace in modern vampire films, but this seems to be its first appearance.) Edlemann investigates, and discovers that vampirism is caused by a blood parasite. But these researches, and the plot in general, are complicated by Dracula's interest in the doctor's beautiful young assistant, Miliza, and further still by the re-entry of the Wolf Man and Frankenstein's monster. The vampiric subplot ends with Dracula once again being wiped out by sunlight, though the other monsters keep up their mischief for another couple of reels.

The bottom of the Universal barrel was finally scraped with *Abbot and Costello Meet Frankenstein* (1948), which is mainly worth mention (a) as the first feature-length vampire spoof or comedy, and (b) as the second and last time Bela Lugosi played Dracula on screen.

The studio did not return to this vein again until 1979, with John Badham's *Dracula*; see below, 'Gorey Details'.

PHANTOM BATS OVER PARIS: SURREALIST VAMPIRES

The Surrealists were bound to be suckers for vampires. A taste for supernatural creatures went hand-in-hand with their admiration for the id-like forces, irrational narrative leaps and general sense of delirium they found in the early cinema, and for the Gothic tradition in English literature, and for the undead-haunted Comte de Lautréamont (see above). There is a (possibly apocryphal) story about André Breton, the founder of the movement, wandering into a screening of *Nosferatu* part-way through its running time and seeing the inter-title which read, 'and when he crossed the bridge, the phantoms came to meet him'. The words struck him with the force of an epiphany, and he simply turned around and left the cinema, feeling as if he were floating six feet off the ground. Whether or not the story is true, Breton would almost certain have known about the film, which had been reviewed by his close friend and fellow Surrealist Robert Desnos.

It is, then, slightly disappointing to note that this keen Surrealist vampophilia did not result in the production of any canonical films, poems or images, save for the superb Victorian bat-gentleman in Max Ernst's *Une Semaine de bonté* (1934), or for a short, remarkable natural history film about vampire bats by Jean Painlevé (1945); the scene in which a bat clamps itself to the nose of a poor guinea pig and feeds is much more distressing than most horror movies.

A STAKE IN THE FUTURE: ENTER THE SCIENCE FICTION VAMPIRES

It is generally agreed that the best, and certainly the most influential vampire fiction of the half-century after Stoker's book was published, is Richard Matheson's *I Am Legend* (1954). Sparse, harsh and compelling, Matheson's novel depicts a future world – the mid-1970s, after some kind of unspecified but obviously terrible war, probably nuclear – in which only one man, the narrator Robert Neville, appears to have survived. By day, he forages for canned food and other useful goods in abandoned stores; by night, he hunkers down in his fortified suburban house, listening to hordes of vampires howling for his blood and stoning his walls and windows. Attentive to the psychological horrors of loneliness, bereavement and despair as well as physical nasties, the book earns its reputation as a first-rate chiller.

It also marks a turning point in the history of vampire fiction. Matheson's vampires – though vulnerable to daylight, to garlic and to wooden stakes, in the approved fashion – are not supernatural beings but the victims of an airborne virus. From 1954 onwards, the idea of vampires as a biological freak rather than creatures from the Pit became one of the staples of the horror genre. (Not just of vampire films, either: George Romero's terrifying zombie flick *Night of the Living Dead* and its sequels all owe something to Matheson.) There have been three film versions to date: *The Last Man on Earth* (1964, starring Vincent Price), *The Omega Man* (1971) and, most recently and expensively, *I Am Legend* (2007), starring Will Smith, which has a terrific first act and a contemptible, happy-ending finale.

Matheson's other substantial contributions to the vampire genre include a much-anthologized short story, 'Drink My Red Blood'; the screenplay for *The Night Stalker* (1971), a highly successful television movie about a vampire hunter, made with the producer and director Dan Curtis; and the screenplay for Curtis's 1973 production of *Dracula*, starring Jack Palance.

New Nails for Old Coffins: Hammer Films and Christopher Lee

Though its budget was minute, and though it takes many liberties with Stoker's property, the first Hammer Films *Dracula* (or, as it is known in the USA, *Horror of Dracula*), directed by Terence Fisher, has a good claim to being one of the three or four best productions of its kind, and certainly one of the most influential. If Bela Lugosi still provides us with the definitive image of the Count, then Christopher Lee runs him a close second. And Lee was a much better actor, both in range and intensity. Compared to the gore and splatter of twenty-first-century vampire flicks, *Dracula* can look like a genteel Merchant Ivory period film. Yet Lee is, as has been well said, the most authentically frightening of all screen Draculas, and the first sudden close-up of his fully vampiric face, fangs bared, eyes blazing red, retains its power to make audiences shriek. It is a tribute to Lee's extraordinary charisma that, even though the Hammer series became sillier and more feeble with the years, his central character was never significantly diminished.

The story of Lee as Dracula begins in the second half of the 1950s, when Hammer – having noticed the box-office power of their *Quatermass* film (1955) and other horrific subjects – bought the remake rights to both the Frankenstein and the Dracula franchises from Universal Pictures. (The rights did not extend to the physical appearance of the monsters, which remained Universal's copyright, and still does.) Lee was cast as the monster in *Curse of Frankenstein*, and the film was an immediate international success, so the studio quickly went on to make its obvious counterpart.

The Hammer *Frankenstein* and *Dracula* movies were the first to be shot in colour – a technical advance which repelled or delighted its first audiences according to their taste. Their *Dracula* was also the first vampire film since *Nosferatu* to show Dracula with fangs – enlarged canines, this time, rather than ratty front teeth. Again, *Dracula* was a huge international hit, and established Lee (born 1922) as a star. Sequels were inevitable – though, oddly, Lee refused to take part in the first few, and only returned to the role after almost a decade.

The essential Christopher Lee/Hammer *Dracula* series comprises seven films:

✝ *Dracula* (1958); also known in the USA as *The Horror of Dracula*.

✝ *Dracula, Prince of Darkness* (1966).

✝ *Dracula Has Risen from the Grave* (1969).

✝ *Taste the Blood of Dracula* (1970).

✝ *The Scars of Dracula* (1970).

✝ *Dracula A.D. 1972* (1972).

✝ *The Satanic Rites of Dracula* (1973); also known as *Count Dracula and the Vampire Brides*.

Outside the Hammer cycle, Lee also appeared as Dracula in *El Conde Dracula* (1970), by Jesus Franco. (Pedro Portabella made a documentary, *Vampir*, about the filming of *El Conde*; Lee appeared in the documentary, reading from the final chapter of Stoker's novel.) And then, for one last time, in *Dracula père et fils* (1976), a French comedy.

Lee also participated in a Swedish documentary (1974) based on *In Search of Dracula* (1972), by Raymond T. McNally and Radu Florescu; Lee narrated, and appeared in a few scenes as Vlad the Impaler.

He also played other vampires:

✝ In the Italian comedy *Tempi duri per i vampiri* – as 'Baron Rodrigo'.
✝ In a Mario Bava film, as 'Lico', who battles Hercules in the underworld.
✝ In a cameo in *The Magic Christian*.

It has been suggested that his character's name in George Lucas's *Star Wars*, 'Count Dooku', is a muffled echo of his vampiric past.

The Lee Dracula Canon: a Survey, in Seven Parts

ONE: *Dracula* (1958, directed by Terence Fisher; written by Jimmy Sangster). There is nothing showy or overtly brilliant about Fisher's direction; on the contrary, it is the very simplicity and elegance of composition that give his film a kind of dignity and quiet, cumulative force. Shot in highly saturated Technicolor, the sets and costumes have a lush, sensual quality – deep blues and reds predominate – that make Dracula's all-black outfit stand out like a dark, defiling stain. Much of the film is played out on small sets, no doubt as a result of the cramped budget, but Fisher makes the wide-screen aspect ratio (often used for grand vistas, not intimate scenes) seem perfectly apt. Going against the grain both of its Universal predecessor and the general conventions of Gothic, much of this *Dracula* is brightly lit, and the rooms of Dracula's castle, far from being the dank cobwebby chambers of decay, are clean and almost cosy.

The screenplay by Jimmy Sangster plays fast and loose with Stoker's novel, simplifying the action considerably, and changing or conflating characters. It is all set during the year 1885, in two neighbouring states somewhere in Central or Eastern Europe (the place names are all Germanic: 'Klausenburg', 'Karlstadt', 'Ingstadt', etc.). After the credit sequence and opening shots – a sculptured eagle, on the ramparts of a castle, then a long, deliberate track down to a tomb, inscribed with the single word DRACULA – we pick up the action in what at first seems to be familiar style, as Jonathan Harker approaches Castle Dracula. However, this Harker is not a solicitor, but a librarian; or, in reality, not a librarian either, but a vampire hunter, come to slay the ancient demon. He is disconcerted by meeting a lightly clad maiden in distress; and then by meeting the exquisitely polite Count himself.

Things thereafter go much as one might expect. The young woman is, of course, a vampire; when Harker stakes her, the body ages into that of a crone. But Dracula escapes . . . in search, we strongly suspect, of Harker's fiancée, Lucy Holmwood, whom he has seen in the portrait that Harker carries with him. Cut to Van Helsing (Peter Cushing), freshly arrived in the nearby village in search of his lost colleague, Harker. Van Helsing makes it to the castle, where he finds Harker's body lying in a tomb; and sporting fangs . . .

Van Helsing returns home, to see his friend Arthur Holmwood, married brother of Harker's fiancée – herself now an anaemic invalid, for reasons that we can easily guess: Dracula is paying her visits by night. (Dr Seward, who is treating her, is an old buffoon.) Van Helsing tries to protect her by strewing her room with garlic, but the maid removes it, and Lucy dies, only to rise again, and to menace the maid's small daughter, Tania. Eventually, Van Helsing manages to stake her. Meanwhile, Dracula has begun laying siege to Holmwood's wife, Mina. He kidnaps her, and takes her back to his castle. Holmwood and Van Helsing give chase; at last, Dracula and Van Helsing fight – a fight won by Van Helsing when he tears open the giant curtains in Dracula's great room, exposing him to solar rays that reduce him to dust, blown away by the wind.

Half a century old now, the film bears its years lightly. Some of the minor acting is less than accomplished, and the rare touches of comic relief (Miles Malleson as an undertaker with a morbid sense of fun) are superfluous, but for the most part it is a taut, handsomely mounted and compelling piece of storytelling, all done without a hint of camp. The dialogue is economical and literate, Peter Cushing has wonderful gravitas as Van Helsing and Lee has never been bettered. Even by himself.

TWO: *Dracula, Prince of Darkness* (1966, directed and written, again, by Terence Fisher and Jimmy Sangster). Parts of the film are every bit as handsomely shot as the first *Dracula*. In other respects; well . . .

The first two or three minutes are a simple reprise of the previous film's final sequence, with a voice-over informing us that this daring act by Van Helsing put an end to Dracula's long reign of terror. Cut to a funeral in the forest: locals, carrying the body of a young girl and a hammer and stake. But this quaint local custom is ruined by the arrival of an angry, unusually rationalist monk, Father Sandor, who will have none of it, and confiscates the corpse.

Next, we encounter two rather irritating English couples, who are on holiday here in the Carpathians. Alan and Helen (Charles Tingwell and Barbara Shelley), and – contemporary audiences would have had no reason to giggle at the characters' names – Charles and Diana (Francis Matthews and Susan Farmer). These tourists run into Father Sandor at a local inn. When he hears that they are planning to go to 'Carlsbad' (presumably no one could be bothered to check that the place name was 'Klausenberg' in the first film), he loses a good part of his fiercely avowed rationalism and warns them away. Naturally, through a combination of dim-wittedness and supernatural intervention, they end up being taken to Castle Dracula by enchanted coach.

The castle seems quite pleasant at first, and its sole inhabitant, a manservant by the name of Klove (a name possibly inspired by the manservant character in Beckett's *Endgame*?), is disarmingly hospitable, if chilly and weird. After a certain amount of stalling, the action really clicks into gear when Klove stabs Alan, strings him up head downwards over an open sarcophagus, cuts his throat and lets the blood gush downwards onto a small pile of ashes. Ashes which form into Dracula. (This sequence, frequently copied, is the film's most telling stroke.) And so the traditional game kicks off once more. After assorted scuffles, which leave Helen vampirized, the survivors flee back to Father Sandor at his monastery. Sandor explains to them that they are safe here, because of the rule that vampires cannot enter a building unless invited.

Tough luck: a character called Ludwig – a Renfield in all but name, given to guzzling flies – lets Dracula in. Dracula, by the way, does not speak a word throughout the entire film. His muteness is never remarked upon. (The gossip is that Lee refused to speak Sangster's dialogue because he considered it too poor.) Poor Helen is staked by the good guys; Dracula kidnaps Diana and flees back to his castle, where the goodies eventually see him off by blasting holes in the ice that covers the river which runs by its foundations. Dracula teeters, then falls into the running water.

And we all know what that does to vampires.

✝HREE: *Dracula Has Risen From The Grave* (1969, directed by Freddie Francis; written by Anthony Hinds) . . . and has apparently recovered his powers of speech; well, to some extent. Lee only appears in about fifteen minutes or so of the total running time, and speaks no more than seven or eight lines, mostly curt and outraged, from 'Who has done this thing?' (i.e. nailed up his castle door with a large metal crucifix), to 'Get that thing [the same crucifix] out of my sight!'

The film's most inventive visual coup comes in its first sequence: the body of a buxom wench, obviously a recent victim of a you-know-what, flops down from a giant church bell like a busty clapper. Jump forward a year or so: the local priest who found the dangling wench has hit the schnapps in a bad way and neglected his clerical duties. Enter a Monsignor (Rupert Davies), with plans to put Dracula's legacy to rest for ever, by exorcizing his castle. Reluctantly, the schnapps-sodden priest escorts his superior up the mountain, but falters on the way. The Monsignor carries out his exorcism, while the elements crash and thunder in sympathetic agonies; the flawed priest tumbles down the mountain, and crashes into a block of ice – inside which we can see the face of Dracula. Blood trickles from the priest's cut head . . . and Dracula is back in business. Or will be in a short while.

Much of the central part of the film takes the form of a domestic comedy-cum-romance; a knockabout idyll that gradually curdles into supernatural violence. Back home from his exorcism, the Monsignor is reunited with his widowed sister-in-law, his beautiful young niece Maria, and her suitor Paul – a humble baker's assistant but also an ambitious scholar, and a loud-mouthed atheist into the bargain. The Monsignor thunders his disapproval, and so sets off a clandestine love affair, complicated by local waitress and good-time-girl Zena (Barbara Ewing), who has an eye for Paul.

Enter, seething with rage, Dracula, with the injured priest now under his thrall. He chomps redheaded Zena, who clearly enjoys the whole thing very much; then turns his attention to Maria, who despite being a blonde and virginal Good Girl, obviously finds Dracula's nip equally irresistible. The tale grows darker: Dracula wearies of Zena and the priest destroys her in the baker's open fire; Dracula kills the Monsignor; Paul tries to stake Dracula, but his attempt fails because he cannot back up his staking with the power of sincere prayer. Dracula takes the mesmerized Maria back to his castle, and has her wrench the crucifix from the door, then throw it down the mountainside. Enter Paul and the priest, who is now recovering his old religious self thanks to some shrewd applications of the cross. Paul and Dracula struggle, and the Count falls down the cliff, to be impaled on the discarded crucifix. This time, the priest backs up the action with prayer, and recites the paternoster in Latin; Dracula convulses, then vanishes. Paul, evidently an atheist no more, holds on to Maria and crosses himself.

The series has, in short, already started to giggle at itself. That Lee's dignified menace survives all of the surrounding tomfoolery – as it does in the subsequent films – is not far short of a miracle . . . Whether photographed in long shot (the sharp diagonal lines of his floor-length cloak rendering him a black isosceles triangle), close-up (green lighting to give his flesh the pallor of decay) or extreme close-up (bloodshot contact lenses), he remains a potent, demonic force.

Note: Director Freddie Francis also made the justly neglected *Count Downe – Son of Dracula* (1973); a comedy of sorts with Ringo Starr.

FOUR: *Taste the Blood of Dracula* (1970, directed by Peter Sasdy; written by Anthony Hinds). Though it trails away disappointingly, indeed disastrously, in its later scenes, this fourth instalment has a very promising beginning. A prologue features an English travelling salesman (played by the well-liked comic actor Roy Kinnear) showing off some of his new wares to a sinister couple of thugs in a stagecoach. They attack him, and throw him from the coach into the night. Howls – of dogs or wolves first, then of other creatures – fill the night, and the man panics. He picks up his bags and runs blindly until finally he is stopped by a terrible sight – in fact, by footage of the death of Dracula from the previous film. He waits until Dracula's gooey blood turns with preternatural rapidity into dust . . .

Cut to the tranquillity of Victorian London, where various respectable middle-class families are leaving church. The next few minutes briskly establish (a) that one of the gentleman shown here enforces strict chastity in his daughter Lucy (Isla Blair), and forbids her ever to see her suitor Paul (Anthony Higgins), and (b) that this gentleman and two local friends are deep-dyed hypocrites, whose 'charitable activities' in the East End are a front for orgies in their favourite brothel. (The brothel scenes are done in lively style, and include the first fully naked breasts of the series.) But their palates are becoming weary of such ordinary depravities, so they are easy targets for a Byronic young nobleman, Lord Courtley, who offers them the ultimate in sensation. Despite their misgivings, they go along with him, and spend a thousand guineas at Kinnear's old curiosity shop for the relics of Dracula, including his dried blood.

The young lord takes them to a remote chapel, where they perform a Satanic mass, and he swills the newly liquid blood of the Count. Then he starts to gag to death. The others panic, and in their fearful frenzies hasten Lord Courtley's demise with a few swift kicks. Then they run, reasonably sure that their crime will not be discovered. But the fallen body in the chapel mutates into Dracula, who vows revenge. The rest of the film consists of his vengeance – killing the fathers and biting their daughters (Sasdy plays up the orgasmic quality of being amorously bitten even more than previous directors had), until he finally perishes from the usual crucifix exposure, and Paul rescues Lucy. Among the unintentionally comic aspects of the film when seen today is that one of the fathers is played by Peter Sallis, now best known as the voice of the mild-mannered, cheese-loving inventor in Nick Park's *Wallace and Gromit* films. 'Cracking plasma, Gromit . . .'

It is high time for this tour to accelerate.

FIVE: *The Scars of Dracula* (1970, directed by Roy Ward Baker). What Peter Sallis is to *Taste the Blood of Dracula*, Dennis Waterman is to *The Scars of Dracula*: viewers who grew up on the British TV series *Minder* will expect Arthur Daley to sidle into view any minute, and try to flog Dracula a load of virgins that fell off the back of a lorry. Unfair; but unavoidable. Not, to be frank, that there is much here to spoil by giggling. A swift summary: Dracula is revived by blood dripped from an obliging bat. Villagers storm his castle and burn some of it down. In revenge, Dracula sends a host of bats to tear their womenfolk to death. A randy young chap named Paul, on the run from an irate daddy, winds up at the castle, where the usual formalities take place – near-fanging by a female vampire, that sort of thing.

Paul tries to escape; Klove, the servant (played by the second Dr Who, Patrick Troughton), makes sure he doesn't, and becomes obsessed with a photograph of Sarah (Jenny Hanly), who is part of a love triangle with Paul and his brother Simon (Dennis Waterman). Sarah and Simon make it to the castle and rumble with the Count, but Klove helps them escape – and is burned with a red-hot poker for his troubles. And so on. This time around, the Count is destroyed by lightning, which strikes a metal spear he is about to use on Simon. Let's just leave it at that.

SIX: *Dracula A.D. 1972* (1972, directed by Alan Gibson). This preposterous tale is interesting mainly for showing that, half a decade after London was pronounced 'swinging' by *Time* magazine, middle-aged film-makers still had not the faintest idea how to portray a 'youth culture' that was already well past its first flush of youth. (By instructive contrast, Donald Cammell's *Performance* – made two years earlier, and by some of the sort of Chelsea people Gibson's film so ludicrously fails to capture – gains in wit, menace and even profundity with the years.) It begins with a prelude in 1872, showing 'Lawrence' (*sic*) Van Helsing seeing off the Count yet again, this time during a wild fight through London on a runaway carriage. This completely jettisons the series' earlier chronologies, but never mind.

Jump to a rather pallid-looking but doggedly swinging London, where Van Helsing's descendant Lorrimer is still fighting occult evil, while his slightly dopey granddaughter Jessica has taken up with a bad crowd, who are rude to their elders and use words like 'scene', 'fuzz' and 'twit'. So bad are they that they are easily tempted by a young blood, name of Johnny Alucard (haven't any of these kids been to the movies?), into staging a black mass, which brings the Count back. The Count starts chomping as usual, and you can guess the rest. Holy water sees him off.

The English horror writer Kim Newman (see Chapter Five) confesses to a guilty love of this film, and it does have a few redeeming features: Peter Cushing's welcome return; a feline, swaggering performance by Christopher Neame as Johnny, who looks and moves a lot like Malcolm McDowell in *A Clockwork Orange*; and, for those boys who reached puberty round about the early 1970s and remember her adverts for a well-known brand of rum, a cameo from the dreamily voluptuous Caroline Munroe. But that's about all.

SEVEN: *The Satanic Rites of Dracula* (1972, directed by Alan Gibson; in the USA, *Count Dracula and his Satanic Bride*). Though not ever as embarrassing as *A.D. 1972*, this is definitely a mess. It issues fair warning in a shoddy credit sequence – tourist shots of London, a cheap graphic of a vampire's outline – and its theme music, which sounds like Vaughan Williams trying to pastiche Isaac Hayes's theme for *Shaft*. Lee's time on screen, sad to say, can barely run to more than fifteen minutes, and in one of his scenes, he doesn't even wear the traditional cloak. Outrage! It starts out as a sort of occult conspiracy thriller, in which the British security services are investigating a Satanic cult that has recruited some of the most powerful men in the realm. The film teeters towards satire, with the discovery that the powerful multinational company Denham is in fact run by Dracula (who speaks, the first time we hear him, in a thick Central European accent, almost but not quite a parody of Lugosi's, though he reverts to Queen's English by the finale; we never learn how he became reincarnated this time). The film then concludes in apocalyptic science fiction, when we learn that Dracula plans to unleash a new strain of bubonic plague, and wipe out all humanity; quite why he wants to destroy his food supply in this way is never quite explained. Van Helsing postulates a 'subconscious' death wish. The Count is thwarted, again, by Van Helsing and an enterprising policeman. Van Helsing lures him into a hawthorn bush, and stakes him. He crumbles; and this time, he stayed crumbled. One of the few redeeming features is that the actress who plays Van Helsing's granddaughter Jessica for this outing is Joanna Lumley, one of Britain's national treasures: here abundantly redheaded, and already with a voice like Belgian truffles.

And so ended the Hammer Draculas. Though not, quite yet, its vampire series.

Other Hammer Vampires

✝ *The Brides of Dracula* (1960) – in which the Count does not appear.
✝ *Kiss of the Vampire* (1962).

The 'Karnstein' trilogy:
✝ *Vampire Lovers* (1970) – based on Le Fanu's *Carmilla*; starring Ingrid Pitt.
✝ *Lust for a Vampire* (1971).
✝ *Twins of Evil* (1971).

✝ *Vampire Circus* (1971).
✝ *Captain Kronos, Vampire Hunter* (1972).
✝ *Twins of Evil* (1972).

And, finally, a co-production with the Shaw Brothers of Hong Kong:
✝ *The Legend of the Seven Golden Vampires* (1974, Roy Ward Baker; also known as *The Seven Brothers Meet Dracula*). Peter Cushing played Van Helsing one last time.

Hammer went bankrupt in 1975. There have been rumours, ever since, that it is about to come back from the dead. For a full and fascinating account of its life and times, see David Pirie's pioneering study *A Heritage of Horror* (revised as *A New Heritage of Horror*, 2008).

THE MONSTROUS REGIMENT OF UNDEAD WOMEN: VAMPIRE LESBIANS

Cinema was relatively slow to pick up on the rich literary heritage of lesbian vampires, except in highly coded forms. Until the late 1950s, only *Dracula's Daughter* (1936) was more or less explicit in showing undead-girl-on-living-girl action. Then came the likes of *Lust of the Vampire* (*I Vampiri*, 1957, directed by Mario Bava; based on the story of Elizabeth Bathory – see Chapter Two) and *Blood and Roses* (1960, directed by Roger Vadim – based on *Carmilla*).

But the genre really took off in the 1970s, with three films from Hammer – the so-called 'Karnstein' trilogy – based, again, on the notorious career of Elizabeth Bathory. Then the contenders come thick and fast. A few highlights:

Valerie and her Week of Wonders (1970, directed by Jaromil Jireš). A truly extraordinary Czech film, deserving a more substantial reputation (it is available on DVDs of varying quality). It was adapted from a novel of 1935 by Vitězslav Nezval, and in turn is said to have been a major influence on the English novelist Angela Carter. The film is, apparently, a great favourite of the Icelandic rock band Sigur Rós.

Daughters of Darkness (1971, directed by Harry Kümel). Considered something of a masterpiece by its admirers (I dissent; apart from other defects, the acting is mostly awful), this stars the art-house darling Delphine Seyrig – in an array of eye-smacking costumes by top designers – as, yet again, the deathless Countess Bathory.

The Hunger (1983, directed by Tony Scott; see Chapter Five). Catherine Deneuve in greedy pursuit of Susan Sarandon.

More recently, films such as *Mark of Lilith* (1986, directed by Bruna Fionda and Polly Gladwin) have been more politically militant than their predecessors, most of which are fairly obviously aimed at heterosexual men with a penchant for such fare.

Vamporn: a Note on Jean Rollin

The French director Jean Rollin (born 1938) has made a career almost exclusively from ultra-low-budget erotic vampire films, many of them with lashings of lesbian content: *Le Viol du vampire* (1968; in the USA, *Rape of the Vampire), La vampire nue* (1970; *The Naked Vampire), Le Frisson des vampires* (1971; *Vampire Thrills), Le Cult des vampires, Requiem pour un vampire, Les Deux Orphelines vampires, La Fiancée de Dracula . . .* and many, many others; he almost certainly belongs in the record books as the man who has made more vampire flicks than anyone. Rollin has also written vampire fiction, and a heavily illustrated critical analysis of his own *oeuvre*.

FIRST BLOOD: CUTE VAMPIRES FOR KIDDIES; OR, FROM COUNT DRACULA TO COUNT DUCKULA

The nightmare gradually becomes familiar; the familiar becomes comfortable; ultimately, the comfortable becomes cute and funny.

The strange route by which Count Dracula and his terrible kind were stripped of all their menace and became cuddly begins in the late 1940s, with the release of *Abbott and Costello Meet Frankenstein* in the USA and, in Britain, with *Old Mother Riley Meets the Vampire* (see 'Bela Lugosi', above). The on-screen characters were amusingly scared by the vampires they bumped into, but audiences were meant to giggle; and they did. After these comedies, most movie vampires went off on a long sabbatical, at least in America. Hollywood made relatively few ventures into vampiric territory in the 1950s and 1960s, preferring on the whole to let the British take over the old Gothic themes (see 'New Nails for Old Coffins', above), and concentrating instead on films about more contemporary mythologies of bug-eyed monsters, nuclear mutations, flying saucers and creatures from the Black Lagoon. The Japanese had Godzilla.

Meanwhile, the new one-eyed monster in the living rooms of Middle America was proving so hungry for audience-pleasing fodder that it started to consume the back catalogues of the movie studios. A new generation of viewers, the original Baby Boomers, first encountered Frankenstein, Dracula and the Wolf Man in the comfort of their own homes, instead of the collective darkness of the movie theatres. These beasts were crammed into small screens; their exploits were cropped at the edges, and punctuated every few minutes with rackety commercials. No wonder these nightmare creations lost much of their awe; no wonder they began to seem almost like members of the family – loveable if eccentric uncles or toothy pets; electronic babysitters. Even quite small children, who still shrieked when the Monster lunged forward, could sense that there was something just a little bit silly going on here. And even fairly mainstream consumers learned the attractions of the once distinctively gay sensibility now known as camp. These old movies are trashy? Sure. Why else would you watch them?

The transformation from horror to farce became complete in 1964, with the launch of a television sitcom called *The Munsters*. (It was produced, in part, by Universal, who held all the visual copyrights to the appearances of their classic horrors.) The conceit was simple: make a straightforward comedy about a mild-mannered, suburban, upper-working-class family, but with one twist: make it a family of monsters – monsters who do not realize that there is anything remotely strange about them. Three of the Munsters were conspicuously vampiric: Grandpa (played by Al Lewis), who wore the full Lugosi fig of evening dress and cape; Lily, the mother and wife, a foxy creature with long black hair and a low-cut shroud (Yvonne de Carlo); and the small son Eddie (Butch Patrick), with pronounced widow's peak and pointy ears.

The humour of *The Munsters* was broad, affable and obvious, like a Gothic *Flintstones*, and often turned on newcomers screaming at the sudden sight of Herman Munster (Fred Gwynne), a Karloffian Frankenstein's monster, thus prompting him to scream back in bewilderment or shock. There were occasional inventive touches, including Grandpa's Hot Rod, a customized coffin car known as the Drag-U-La. The series ran for seventy episodes until 1966, when ratings fell off sharply. It spawned several feature films, comic strips and merchandising, a sequel series *The Munsters Today* (1988–91) and persistent rumours of a high-budget movie update. The world does not need one.

An almost exact contemporary of The *Munsters, The Addams Family*, was screened by ABC television from September 1964 to April 1966, in a run of sixty-four episodes. Loosely inspired by the ghoulish *New Yorker* cartoons of Charles Addams, the series was a shade or two more sophisticated than *The Munsters*, especially in its hints at the still-torrid sex lives of the leading characters, Gomez and Morticia. Although none of the characters is explicitly a vampire, Morticia (Carolyn Jones) has the long black hair and long, clinging black gown traditionally associated with Brides of Dracula, and her hobbies – such as raising flesh-eating plants – would make her welcome at any vampiric gathering. Though, again, the humour was fairly mild, the show flirted with poor taste more overtly than *The Munsters*, and had a touch of two of surrealist fancy that may have been due to the influence of Groucho Marx, a good friend of its producer.

Cereal Killer and Vampire Varmint

For a whole generation, vampires now meant giggles as much as shrieks, and the way was open for the whole genre to be both literally and metaphorically de-fanged, and sent off to play in the nursery. One overpowering sign that the times really had a-changed was the advent of the breakfast cereal Count Chocula – the invention of a young advertising copywriter, Laura Levine, who was given the task of branding two new products from the General Mills food company, one with strawberry and marshmallows, one with chocolate. She hunted around for famous double-acts of the past . . . and came up with 'Frankenberry' and 'Count Chocula'. The appearance of the Count on the packaging has changed over the last three decades or so, and nowadays would not alarm the most timid tyke.

From the 1970s onwards, the proliferation of vampire-themed books, comics, cartoons, television programmes and films has been so great that there is no point in trying to be compendious. (But see the 'Dime-Store Draculas' sections below for a few outstanding examples.) Soon after it was launched, the educational programme *Sesame Street* introduced a Dracula-based character, the Count, who has a thick Transylvanian accent and teaches small children – well, what did you expect? – to count. There were several spin-off books and other products.

In 1979, the writer James Howe introduced the world to what probably remains the single most cuddly bloodsucker of all time – Bunnicula, the vampire rabbit. Except, of course, that Bunnicula is a vegetarian, and only sucks the juices of salad stuff. Bunnicula is adopted by the Monroe family, who find him at a cinema showing *Dracula*. They are surprised to find that he sleeps all day, and has two suspiciously fang-like front teeth. It is the family dog, Chester, who discovers that Bunnicula has been raiding the refrigerator by night; when the Monroes wake up one morning and witness a fearful sight –

a white tomato, drained of all its red juice – there is only one conclusion. They tackle him with garlic, till he nearly starves . . . and then relent. Bunnicula's adventures continued on television and across a number of sequels, including one with the toothsome title *The Celery Stalks at Midnight.*

For British children, and quite a number of adults, the wittiest and best-loved of all such kiddie vampire fare is the animated series *Count Duckula*, which was first broadcast in 1988 and ran for sixty-five episodes, all now available on DVD. The hero, a fanged green duck in traditional vampire cape, has a complicated back-story. He has died many times, and been reincarnated each century thanks to a magic ritual, performed 'when the moon is in the eighth house of Aquarius'. Duckula retains very few memories from life to life, and has variously been a scientist, an artist, an Egyptologist, a gambler . . . but, in each incarnation, always a Vicious Vampire Duck.

But something has gone wrong with Duckula's latest incarnation. Thanks to some bungling at his rebirthing ritual, he was revived not with blood but with tomato ketchup. As a result, he is a harmless vegetarian (his favourite food: broccoli sandwiches), who dreams mainly of fame and fortune as an entertainer – something that makes him the constant despair of his butler, Igor, a lugubrious vulture who keeps trying to convert him into a proper vampire. Meanwhile, Duckula has a nemesis, his own Van Helsing, in the form of Doctor Von Goosewing, a mad scientist who stubbornly refuses to notice that Duckula isn't hurting anyone these days.

Duckula – voiced by the popular comedy actor David Jason – inhabits the standard vampire's castle, except that Castle Duckula has the power to transport itself anywhere in the world for a limited period; there are some hints that it may be semi-sentient. The series boasted a large cast of supporting characters, mainly in bird form, and some delicious ideas, from Duckula's family motto *'Per Ardua ad Sanguina'* (oddly translated as 'work for blood'), to the titles of the episodes: 'Translyvanian Homesick Blues', for example, an allusion to Bob Dylan's 'Subterranean Homesick Blues'. There are rumours that Count Duckula may be returning in the form of a full-length feature from the estimable Aardman company. We can only pray.

VAMPS ON CAMPUS: THE VAMPIRE AS ACADEMIC

One of the best vampire novels of the period between Richard Matheson (1950s) and Anne Rice (1970s) is the work of a mainstream novelist, Simon Raven, who usually specialized in mordant social satire. *Doctors Wear Scarlet* – the title wittily alludes to the dress instructions on an invitation to a college feast – concerns the exploits of Richard Fountain, a classics don of Lancaster College, Cambridge, who comes back from a research trip in Greece (note the Byronic connection) strangely transformed . . .

Raven's novel was published in 1960; a film version was released in 1969, featuring Peter Cushing in the role of Dr Walter Goodrich. The idea of academics as vampires has been reprised several times: see, for example, Suzy McKee Charnas's story-cycle *The Vampire Tapestry* (1980), in which the sympathetic vampire lead is Dr Edward Weyland, a brilliant and highly regarded anthropologist; and Abel Ferrara's film *The Addiction*, discussed in Chapter Five.

BLOOD AND SUDS: VAMPIRE SOAP

For Americans of a certain age, the one vampire fiction to rival *Dracula* for recognition value is the long-running Gothic soap opera *Dark Shadows*, a creation of the producer Dan Curtis, which ran daily on ABC television from 1966 to 1971 (and was revived in 1991) – some 1,200 episodes in all. It rated poorly at first, but took off when the producers introduced a vampire character, Barnabas Collins (played by Jonathan Frid) in April 1967. Almost overnight, the show became a hit – about 20 million people tuned in regularly – and Frid became a star, with a female fan club to rival Lugosi's in the 1930s. Barnabas Collins was a brooding, anxious and largely sympathetic character – an important transitional figure in the long march from Count Dracula to Stephanie Meyer's 'nice' vampires.

There were countless spin-offs, including thirty-three novels, a comic book (precociously breaking the Comics Code, which banned vampires – see below), games, LPs and two feature films: *House of Dark Shadows* and *Night of Dark Shadows* (1970 and 1971, both directed by Dan Curtis). Its influence on American popular (and high) culture has been immense. (The English novelist Matt Thorne, a latter-day scholar and fan of the show, has, for example, pointed out numerous references to it in Donna Tartt's novel *The Little Friend*.) There are reports that Tim Burton is planning to make a feature film, with Johnny Depp in the Barnabas Collins role.

HUMOUR IN A JUGULAR VEIN

Dance of the Vampires (1967; also known as *The Fearless Vampire Killers, or: Pardon Me, But Your Teeth Are in My Neck*) was cinema's first full-blooded, full-length vampire comedy (we can guiltlessly discount the likes of *Old Mother Riley Meets the Vampire* and the *Munsters* spin-offs), and was also the first vampire film since Dreyer's to be made by a major European director: Roman Polanski, who in 1967 was one of the hottest young talents to have fled the East. He acts in the film as 'Alfred', the naive, often bumbling assistant to the vampire hunter Professor Abronius. Even admirers of the film are quick to admit that it is not very funny any more – the humour tends to the obvious, the slapstick can be tiresome and gags about gay vampires no longer seem naughty enough to raise a smirk. But the film's most famous pay-off still raises a chuckle: threatened in traditional style by a crucifix, a conspicuously Jewish vampire (the endearing English actor

Alfie Bass) sneers, 'Have you got the wrong vampire!'

Funny or not, the film remains very handsome indeed – much of it is set in a remote, snowbound hotel and a grand nearby castle – with one set piece: a lavish vampire ball, that, only slightly tweaked, might have made a splendid finale for a more conventional horror film. Ferdy Mayne plays the villain, Count Krolock. There has recently been a musical version, staged in Vienna with a score and lyrics by Jim Steinman, best known as the man who wrote the rock anthems for Meatloaf.

Yes, We Have No Sferatu

Some of the better-known, if not necessarily better, vampire parodies, comedies and spoofs since *Dance of the Vampires*:

Blood for Dracula (1973, directed by Paul Morissey). Also known as *Andy Warhol's Dracula*. Udo Kier plays a modern-day Count who is facing a novel problem; he needs the blood of virgins but, thanks to the sexual revolution, the commodity is in short supply. He travels to Italy, in the hope that a Catholic country will still be enforcing chastity, but his schemes are thwarted by the priapic activities of a stud (Joe Dallesandro, the Warhol 'superstar') who always beats him to it, and leaves him vomiting deflowered blood. An oddity.

Love at First Bite (1979, directed by Stan Dragoti). The handsome George Hamilton plays the Dracula character sauvely, in a style said to be very closely modelled on Lugosi's stage performances. The conceit is that Dracula is forcibly relocated from Communist Romania (we see him shouting at wolves: 'Children of the night – shut up!') to Manhattan, at the height of the disco craze.

Once Bitten (1985, directed by Howard Storm). Features Lauren Hutton as the vampire, and the profoundly irritating Jim Carrey in one of his earliest roles.

Vampires in Havana (1985, directed by Juan Padron). An animated comedy; see Chapter Five.

Fright Night (1985, directed by Tom Holland). In fact, somewhere between a comedy and a straight horror film. It was the first feature to spend more than a million dollars on special effects, though to jaded twenty-first-century eyes they no longer look all that impressive. William Ragsdale is the teenage boy who thinks, rightly, that his new neighbour is a bloodsucker; Chris Sarandon the vampiric neighbour; and Roddy McDowell is the washed-up star of old horror movies who finds himself forced to play Van Helsing for real. There was a sequel, imaginatively entitled *Fright Night II*, in 1988.

Dracula, Dead and Loving It (1995, directed by Mel Brooks). Painfully unfunny, on the whole, with none of the half-loving, half-mocking spirit of *Young Frankenstein*. (It did, however, provide the heading for this subsection. Credit where due.) But it's not without interest as a kind of anthology of vampire movie clichés, since it spoofs any number of vampire films, including one which was a spoof in the first place: *Dance of the Vampires*. The 'children of the night' joke in this one involves, as one might have expected, bat guano: 'Children of the night – what a mess they make!'

BLOOD BROTHERS: AFRICAN-AMERICANS AS VAMPIRES

An almost inevitable product of the early 1970s 'Blaxploitation' era of American cinema, *Blacula* (1972, directed by William Crain) is the first major vampire flick to boast a black hero/villain. The back story is not bad: we learn that Count Dracula (Charles McCauley) numbered among his crimes an investment in the slave trade, and once put an African prince, Mamuwalde, under a curse. Mamuwalde remains imprisoned in his coffin until a brace of gay interior decorators bring the box back to modern Los Angeles. The film starred a Shakespearean actor, William Marshall, who brought it a dignity it did not otherwise deserve. It was hugely profitable for American International – in fact, it made them more than any of their previous productions – so they naturally went on to make a sequel: the forgettable *Scream, Blacula, Scream* (1973). *Blacula* also inspired, if that is the appropriate term, *Black Vampire* (1973, directed by Bill Gunn).

Since Eddie Murphy's *Vampire in Brookyln* (1995, directed by Wes Craven) was such a conspicuous flop, the most famous black vampire today is the comic-book super-hero Blade.

DIME-STORE DRACULAS: VAMPIRE COMICS, 1970-80

The golden age of American horror comics was in the years 1950–2, when literally hundreds of different titles were being churned out, and being bought in their millions by gleefully morbid adolescents. This explosion of gory fare promoted yet another in that long and tiresome series of moral panics and crackdowns that had dogged the medium (see David Hajdu's *The Ten-Cent Plague* (2008) for a solid, detailed history of these censorship wars). This all came to a crashing halt in October 1954, when the industry adopted the Comics Code – which, among other restraints, banned the depiction of vampires and other horrific or supernatural creatures. The key paragraph stated that:

> Scenes dealing with, or instruments associated with walking dead, torture, vampires and vampirism, ghouls, cannibalism and werewolfism are prohibited.

And so the vampires were banished, until the very late 1960s.

Before that date, there had been some softening-up moves. Since the Comics Code did not extend to movie fanzines, influential magazines such as *Famous Monsters of Filmland* were free to publish as many horror-movie stills as they liked, so they started to run strips, too. Mild comedy-horror stories like *The Munsters'* spin-offs also slipped effortlessly past the censors. In 1969, further challenges came in the form of a *Dark Shadows* comic, and then by a slinky vampire chick from outer space, *Vampirella*, whose adventures were as humorous and romantic as they were scary. In the climate of the Sixties, the old Cold War constraints felt more annoying than ever, and the time was ripe for reform, if not revolution. A mild revision of the code in January 1971 made a few important concessions; but not enough for some artists.

The vastly successful company Marvel Comics, under the leadership of the liberal Stan Lee, took the battle forwards by introducing the character of 'Morbius, the Living Vampire' in *The Amazing Spider-Man* (issue 101, October 1971). Strictly speaking, Morbius – previously Dr Michael Morbius, a Nobel Prize-winning biochemist – was not a vampire but a mortal possessed of vampire-like powers, thanks to a mishap involving vampire bats and electric shock. They got away with it, Morbius became a permanent character in the Marvel mythology, and the company went on to launch *Tomb of Dracula*, which ran for seventy issues, and brought Stoker's creation into the modern world.

It was in the pages of *Tomb of Dracula* (issue 10, July 1973) that Marvel introduced the character of Blade the Vampire Hunter, created by Marv Wolfman (see Chapter Five, on the *Blade* trilogy of films). More vampire comics appeared in the course of the 1970s – *Lilith, the Daughter of Dracula* (1974), and DC Comics's *Man-Bat* – but by the end of the decade the public appetite for such fare was going into one of its periodic declines. *Tomb of Dracula* was wound up in 1979, and, with a few exceptions, things fell fairly quiet until the early 1990s.

KING VAMPIRE

If one had to nominate a well-known vampire novel that is at once more frightening, more carefully wrought, and (one might argue) better written than Stoker's, the safest choice would probably be Stephen King's *Salem's Lot* (1975). It was only his second novel and, though he has touched less directly on the vampire theme, remains his major venture to date into classic Stoker territory. (Too good to better?) It is, of its kind, a masterpiece, largely because King allows himself the time and space to create an entire community – the small Maine town of Salem's (Jerusalem's) Lot – sketching in a large and varied cast of characters from nerdy schoolchildren and distraught teenage mothers to burned-out retirees and drunks, all in swift, deft, entirely convincing strokes. One hesitates to call it Dickensian, exactly, but Dickens would definitely have understood what King was up to. (King, an unpretentious fellow, has admitted that he was not really thinking of *Bleak House* or *Our Mutual Friend* when building his doomed town. He was thinking of the best-seller *Peyton Place*, by Grace Metalious. Hence the gag that the novel should really have been called *Satan Place*.) Another way of putting this: *Salem's Lot* is perhaps less a 'vampire novel' than a novel with vampires.

With all the elements of a real world thus secured, King lets the supernatural seep in; in tiny sips at first, then more and more rapidly. The pages which describe the town's turning point – the night when the new vampire population reaches critical mass, and goes on an unstoppable murderous spree – are thrillingly well done. And King's Dracula figure, Mr Barlow (the novelist says that he was inspired by *Dracula* and by E. C. Comics), may well be the most terrifying vampire ever.

It was first filmed for television in 1979 by Tobe Hooper (notorious as the director of the original *Texas Chainsaw Massacre*. Hooper's other major contribution to vampire cinema is *Life Force*, aka *Space Vampires*, adapted from a novel by Colin Wilson). Within the timid conventions available to US television in the 1970s, it's not too bad. David Soul stars as the leading character, a traumatized, recently bereaved young writer who comes back to the town where he spent part of his childhood to exorcize some old demons, and finds that the place has some literal demons to tackle. There is one truly memorable image – a child vampire, floating in mid-air outside a bedroom window at night, scratching at the panes and whining to be let in. But the whole production is marred by flat, dull 1970s lighting, an indifferent supporting cast, and a spirit of self-censorship that keeps King's real horrors firmly at bay.

The Larry Cohen film *A Return to Salem's Lot* (1987) has few points of contact with King's original.

SILENT NIGHTS: DIFFERENTLY ABLED VAMPIRES

Of the many, many productions which have swiped the Stokerian suffix '-ula' (including the gay porno movie *Dragula*), few have been as unpredictable as *Deafula* (1975), a low-budget, black and white feature written by and starring the deaf actor Peter Wolf. All of the characters in the film communicate with each other in sign language, their exchanges being artlessly dubbed for the benefit of the hearing.

AUNTIE DRACULA

It has often been said that the most faithful screen adaptation of Stoker's novel to date is the modestly budgeted, three-hour version produced by the BBC in 1977. This may be so, but the production does take some liberties. Lucy and Mina are now sisters (a revision which, among other things, removes the element of class distinction between them; in the novel, and many films, Lucy is posher than her friend), and live under the same roof with their mother, Mrs Westenra. The aristocratic Arthur Holmwood has been excised, leaving only his surname behind; so Lucy's suitor is now a Texan, name of Quincey P. Holmwood. There are also any number of minor adjustments, some pointless (Van Helsing making cocoa), some interesting (Renfield quoting Blake). Directed by Philip Saville, and written by Gerald Savory, the production is marred by some cheap and ugly special effects, and by rather pallid performances by the younger cast members. But Louis Jourdan makes a very fine Count, handsome and urbane save for his incongruously hairy hands; Frank Finlay, with a wig that makes him resemble Harpo Marx, is a witty and entertaining Van Helsing; and Jack Shepherd gives an outstanding performance as Renfield. When raving, Renfield has never been so frightening; when grasping for his sanity, never so tragic. What an actor!

GOREY DETAILS: DRACULA GOES BROADWAY, AGAIN

In 1977, a revised version of *Dracula* by Deane and Balderston was relaunched on Broadway. It starred Frank Langella as a strikingly handsome, dashing, romantic – in a word, Byronic – Count. As Langella noted with some bemusement, the role suddenly made him a sex symbol, constantly mobbed by female admirers. Apart from Langella, the production's major selling point was its striking, predominantly black and white production design (and costumes) by that sublime and irreplaceable genius, Edward Gorey. Reviews of everything about the production save Gorey's work – which won awards – tended towards the sniffy, but the box office did not suffer at all, and the production went on with a series of prominent actors in the title role.

Alas, when John Badham took on the job of adapting this vehicle for a high-budget movie for Universal, a spirit of caution and realism prevailed, and all of Gorey's designs were thrown out. Shot largely on location in Cornwall, and with Lawrence Olivier as Van Helsing, the

1979 *Dracula* is a perfectly respectable piece of work, with one or two passable ideas: it ends with Dracula on board a ship, with his enemies close behind him, being caught up in the rigging and burning in the sunlight.

Gorey fans will be pleased to hear that his *Dracula Toy Theater* (a cardboard model of the Broadway set, complete with cardboard characters for popping out, propping up and shuffling about) is still available at a reasonable price, as are other memorabilia of the Broadway show.

DEATH'S HEAD REVISITED: HERZOG'S DRACULA

In 1979, Werner Herzog, one of the leading lights of the New German Cinema movement (and, from the perspective of the twenty-first century, probably its hardiest and most enduring talent), chose to remake Murnau's classic under the slightly modified title of *Nosferatu: Phantom der Nacht*, with his long-term alter ego and 'best fiend' Klaus Kinski in the vampire role. The film divides audiences: some consider it a masterpiece, equal if not superior in stature to its distinguished forebear; others – probably a majority – find it glum, slow, self-indulgent, and horribly boring. The musical score – on the one hand Wagner's *Das Rheingold* and the 'Sanctus' from Gounod's *St Cecilia Mass*, on the other hand noodlings from the avant-garde band Popul Vuh – helps thicken the pervasive sense of misery. Indeed, one thing that both audience factions might agree on as crucial to proceedings is the film's general air of melancholia, and its repeated emphasis on Dracula's immortal condition as one of tormenting loneliness. Kinski – done up in Shreck-like make-up, with impractically long nails, a bald head and frontal fangs – suffers emotional agonies before our eyes as no movie vampire has suffered them before. Oh, how he suffers.

Many of the details of Herzog's film are familiar from Murnau, including the Teutonic settings for the film's second and third acts, and

Dracula's plague ship, which shows up in Wismar, Harker's home town, with its freight of rather incongruously cute white rats (a detail which often raises giggles or fond cooing). But the film also contains many of Herzog's own innovations. For no obvious reason, Herzog renames the characters, so that they once again appear as they did in Stoker's book. He also deviates in odd ways from both Stoker and Murnau, for example by making Van Helsing a sceptic, and somewhat slow on the uptake into the bargain, and by having Lucy now as the one who fights back by crumbling the Host into Dracula's coffins. Finally, Jonathan Harker, still turned vampire, survives Dracula's ultimate staking and heads off on horseback across a bleak sea coast, presumably to carry vampirism to other lands. (An unexpected echo, as many people noticed, of Polanski's 1967 film.) For vampire buffs, this is all rather interesting heresy, but one can sympathize with those who are left cold or irritated.

There is a scholarly BFI monograph on Herzog's film by S. S. Prawer, an authority on Weimar cinema; Prawer notes the presence in the film of many German Romantic motifs, including the *Fussreise*, or journey on foot, undertaken by Harker. Herzog's film also spawned a largely forgotten sequel, of sorts: *Nosferatu in Venice* (1988, directed by Augusto Caminito). Kinski reprised his vampire role, this time with a great mane of long white hair – a detail which, in a small way, returns to Stoker.

FIVE

THE LADIES AND THE VAMPS:
1980 TO INFINITY AND BEYOND

FROM ANNE RICE TO STEPHANIE MEYER,
VIA BUFFY SUMMERS

In which more and more vampires become sympathetic outsiders,
action heroes, and romantic heart-throbs; and, in the end,
Vampire Love conquers all

Twenty-Five Notable Vampire Films (plus Sequels) Since 1980

✝ *The Hunger* (1983, directed by Tony Scott).

✝ *Vampire Hunter D* (1985, animation, directed by Tayoo Ashida).

✝ *The Lost Boys* (1987, directed by Joel Schumacher).

✝ *Near Dark* (1987, directed by Kathryn Bigelow).

✝ *Vampire's Kiss* (1989, directed by Robert Bierman).

✝ *Innocent Blood* (1992, directed by John Landis).

✝ *Buffy, the Vampire Slayer* (1992, directed by Fran Rubel Kuzui).

✝ *Bram Stoker's Dracula* (1992, directed by Francis Ford Coppola).

✝ *Cronos* (1993, directed by Guillermo del Toro).

✝ *Interview with the Vampire* (1994, directed by Neil Jordan)
followed by *Queen of the Damned* (2002, directed by Michael Rymer).

✝ *Nadja* (1994, directed by Michael Almereyda).

✝ *The Addiction* (1995; directed by Abel Ferrara).

✝ *From Dusk Till Dawn* (1996, directed by Roberto Rodriguez)
followed by *From Dusk Till Dawn 2: Texas Blood Money* (1999,
directed by Scott Spiegel)
> and *From Dusk Till Dawn 3: The Hangman's Daughter* (2000,
> directed by P. J. Pesce).

✝ *Blade* (1998, directed by Stephen Norrington)
followed by *Blade II* (2002, directed by Guillermo del Toro)
> and *Blade: Trinity* (2004, directed by David S. Goyer).

✝ *The Wisdom of Crocodiles* (1999, directed by Po-Chih Leong)

✝ *Shadow of the Vampire* (2000, directed by E. Elias Merhige)

✝ *Dracula 2000* (2000, directed by Patrick Lussier; in the UK, *Dracula 2001*)
> followed by *Dracula II: Ascension* (2002, directed by Patrick Lussier)
> and *Dracula III: Legacy* (2003, directed by Patrick Lussier).

✝ *Night Watch* (2004, directed by Timur Bekmambetov)
followed by *Day Watch* (2006, directed by Timur Bekmambetov)
> and *Twilight Watch* (scheduled for 2009; directed by Timur
> Bekmambetov).

✝ *Underworld* (2003, directed by Len Wiseman)
followed by *Underworld: Evolution* (2006, directed by Len Wiseman)
> and *Underworld: Rise of the Lycans* (2009, directed by Patrick
> Tatopoulos).

✝ *Dracula: Pages from a Virgin's Diary* (2002, directed by Guy Maddin).

✝ *Van Helsing* (2004, directed by Stephen Sommers).

✝ *30 Days of Night* (2007, directed by David Slade).

✝ *I Am Legend* (2007, directed by Francis Lawrence).

✝ *Let the Right One In* (2008, directed by Tomas Alfredson; an English
language remake, *Let Me In*, is due in 2010).

✝ *Twilight* (2008, directed by Catherine Hardwicke).

Biting at the Box Office

According to Box Office Mojo, the twenty top-grossing vampire films since 1978 are as follows (in dollars; not adjusted for inflation):

1. *Twilight*	186,972,000
2. *Van Helsing*	120,177,084
3. *Interview with the Vampire*	105,264,608
4. *Bram Stoker's Dracula*	82,522,790
5. *Blade II*	82,348,319
6. *Blade*	70,087,718
7. *Underworld: Evolution*	62,318,875
8. *Blade Trinity*	52,411,906
9. *Underworld*	51,970,690
10. *Love at First Bite*	43,885,000
11. *30 Days of Night*	39,568,996
12. *Dracula 2000*	33,022,767
13. *Underworld: Rise of the Lycans*	32,784,000
14. *The Lost Boys*	32,222,567
15. *Queen of the Damned*	30,336,800
16. *From Dusk Till Dawn*	25,836,616
17. *Fright Night*	24,922,237
18. *John Carpenter's Vampires*	20,308,772
19. *Dracula* (1979)	20,158,736
20. *Vampire in Brooklyn*	19,751,736

IF YOU S†AKE US, DO WE NO† BLEED?

The irresistible rise of Anne Rice, and her sympathetic vampires

One of the world's best-selling authors – her novels are reckoned to have sold some 100 million copies worldwide – Anne Rice (born

1941) is, to date, the single most influential contributor to vampire mythology since Stoker himself. (Her eminence has recently been challenged by Stephanie Meyer, but that story is still unfolding.) She was a relatively late starter in fiction, and did not publish her debut volume *Interview with the Vampire* until 1976, though she had completed the text in 1973, and had written a short story of the same name as early as 1969. Though the book was a major hit, she moved away from vampiric subject matter for almost a decade, writing other novels both under the name Anne Rice (*The Feast of All Saints, Cry to Heaven*), and a string of erotic novels with a strong sado-masochistic component under the nom de plume of A. N. Roquelaure.

Rice came back to the territory of *Interview* with *The Vampire Lestat* (1985), which brought the supporting character of Lestat de Lioncourt to centre stage, and was every bit, or bite, as successful as its predecessor. *Lestat* was followed by three further novels in what had now become a series, known as the 'Vampire Chronicles': *The Queen of the Damned* (1988), *The Tale of the Body Thief* (1992) and *Memnoch the Devil* (1995), at which point she alarmed her increasingly avid fans by saying that there would be no more. But she soon relented and wrote – under the group heading of 'New Tales of the Vampires' – *Pandora* (1998) and, in the same series, *Vittorio the Vampire* (1999).

Meanwhile, she picked up the threads of the 'Vampire Chronicles' with:

✝ *The Vampire Armand* (1998).

✝ *Merrick* (2000).

✝ *Blood and Gold* (2001).

✝ *Blackwood Farm* (2002).

✝ *Blood Canticle* (2003).

In 1998, after an adulthood passed mainly as an atheist (apart from a flirtation with Mormonism – the religion of Stephanie Meyer, author of *Twilight*), Rice returned to the Catholic Church she had abandoned in her youth; and, in 2004, announced that she would write no more vampire fiction, and would instead devote her fictional talents to Christian themes. This dismayed many of her readers, who tend towards the fanatical – Ms Rice was driven to move away from New Orleans, long before Katrina, by the hordes of would-be disciples who came and camped out on her lawn. Others, who have found her fiction progressively less readable (and, to be frank, somewhat purple and irritating in the first place), have borne the news with greater stoicism.

Rice's main significance, other than as a publishing phenomenon, is (a) that she dreamed up and made current an intensely sympathetic, almost worshipful version of the vampire – usually, though not always, male and with a heavy dash of androgyny (her undead are often closer to Barnabas Collins than to Graf Orlok; she even spoke of them as being a kind of damaged archangel), and (b) that she made her home town, New Orleans, almost as closely identified with vampirism as Transylvania has been since *Dracula* appeared. Any number of recent vampire fictions have been set in or near the Crescent City; the best of them is probably *Fevre Dream* (see below).

The feature film of *Interview with the Vampire*, directed by Neil Jordan, was finally released in 1994, after a long and tangled route to the screen which had begun as early as 1976, when Paramount took out a ten-year option on the book. Rice initially resisted the decision to cast Tom Cruise as Lestat, since she considered him, among other things, insufficiently androgynous, but eventually came round. Jordan's film was a whopping hit, and is in many ways outstanding, not least for the lush, tenebrous cinematography of Philippe Rousselot, and some wonderfully staged set pieces – a burning plantation house, a Parisian 'Vampire Theatre', deep catacombs . . . Jordan's film flirts so openly with taboo subjects, including necrophilia, that it eventually becomes far more disturbing than the bloodiest of splatter flicks. It also boasts a strikingly precocious performance, miles away from the bland and wholesome roles she has favoured as an adult, by Kirsten Dunst as Claudia, the unaging child vampire – a malevolent moppet with perpetual curls and dimples. Cruise, too, was much more convincing – elegant, menacing, bitingly sardonic – in the role than sceptics had expected.

By contrast to Jordan's accomplishment, the feature film of *The Queen of the Damned* (2002) – about the adventures of Lestat (here, Stuart Townsend) as a rock star – was rubbish.

There have been countless spin-offs from Rice's creations. Sir Elton John attempted a musical version of *Lestat*, with lyrics by Bernie Taupin. Despite decent notices and a reasonably healthy premiere run in San Francisco at the end of 2005, it lasted for only a month at the Palace Theater on Broadway, in May 2006, after receiving mainly tepid to poor reviews. (The cast album has yet to be released.) There was also a ballet version of *Interview*, staged in Prague (1997) and any number of rock songs inspired by the mythos. The most famous is Sting's 'Moon Over Bourbon Street'.

LAND OF THE FREE, HOME OF THE GRAVE

Two of the most well-regarded vampire novels from the early 1980s are also set in the United States.

Vamps in the City of Angels

They Thirst by Robert R. McCammon (1981) is out of print, and likely to remain so as the author does not wish it to be republished, but is nonetheless regarded by cognoscenti as a highly superior contribution to the genre. Vampires plan to take over Los Angeles as the first stepping stone towards world domination; a motley collection of mortals attempts to foil their plan. Among the Bad Guys: Prince Conrad Vulkan, a 700-year-old Hungarian vampire who still looks like a teenager, and in some respects still acts like one; Kobra, a Hell's Angel recruited by Vulkan to run his army; Walter Benefield, a serial killer otherwise known as 'The Roach'; and a figure called 'The Headmaster', who is probably Satan.

Vamps on the Old Mississippi

Fevre Dream, by George R. R. Martin (1983), now firmly established as one of the high-water marks of vampire fiction, is available in the Fantasy Masterworks imprint from Gollancz. On its first appearance, it was described as a cross between Mark Twain and Bram Stoker, and, though pat, that remains a reasonable evocation of its charms.

FOPS WITH FANGS: NEW ROMANTIC VAMPIRES

Tony Scott's well-known film *The Hunger* (1983) was based on a much less well known novel (1981) by Whitley Strieber. The film stars Catherine Deneuve, Susan Sarandon and David Bowie. Set in modern-day New York, it depicts an emotional crisis in the life – or, rather, the long undeath – of Miriam Blaylock, a wealthy, patrician, bisexual vampire (played by Deneuve) whose blood-stock is so pure that she is practically immortal. Alas, her fellow vampire and lover John (Bowie) is of less top-notch provenance, and is starting to crumble at an alarming rate. Miriam seeks out a medical scientist, Dr Sarah Roberts (Sarandon), who might be able to help, but soon finds this gorgeous woman irresistible. Before long, they are lovers – cue lots of 'tasteful' lesbian erotica, dressed up with Delibes – so Miriam chains her poor old lover up in a coffin in the attic. Where, we discover, she has also stashed the remains of his predecessors in her affections. Sarah, now a vampire herself, struggles to cast off the tyrannous appetites that have been quickened in her.

The movie is flashily directed in the manner that Scott would continue to exploit throughout the 1980s and beyond with *Top Gun* and so on – lots of eye-scorching backlighting – though it fails to match its style with much in the way of emotional substance. For some reason, most audiences responded to it excitedly, and it did help establish an entirely new, non-Transylvanian mode of Vampire chic, cold-edged, sharply dressed and thoroughly modern.

Incidentally, *The Hunger* is sometimes said to have been one of the influences on the then-emerging Goth movement in the UK and elsewhere. It opens with a nightclub scene in which the Goth/industrial band Bauhaus are playing their 1979 hit 'Bela Lugosi's Dead'.

BETTER RED THAN UNDEAD: CUBAN VAMPIRES

Vampiros en la Habana (1987, directed by Juan Padrón; *Vampires in Havana*), a feature-length animated film which is about as innocent of Marxist intent as any product of the Cuban film industry in its day could be, has a crude graphic style and still cruder sense of humour; but only a prig could fail to find at least some of it amusing, if not downright funny. The plot is complex and extremely daft.

Set mostly in 1933, it turns on the idea that a vampire mad scientist, Wolfgang Amadeus von Dracula, has developed a potion which makes vampires immune to daylight. Exiled in Havana for reasons that need not be spelled out, he raises his son Joseph, aka Pepe, aka Pepito, on monthly doses of the stuff. Pepe grows up to be a jazz trumpeter, and a plucky member of the rebellion against General Machado. Meanwhile, the bad guys are closing in. A consortium of Euro-vamps is after the formula, which they plan to market as sunblock – 'Vampisol'. But the vampire gangsters of Chicago want the formula for their own ends . . .

Meanwhile, Pepe's love life is vexed. It is part of his revolutionary duty to seduce the wife of the local chief of police, but his fiancée Lola is understandably jealous. The Evil Vampires arrive by sea, and soon the whole town is pinging with silver bullets. The caper comes to an unexpected end when it is discovered that years of guzzling the potion have turned Pepe human; and what self-respecting vampire wants that? Anyway, Pepe is about to blow the whole thing wide open, by transmitting the secret formula for the potion as the lyrics to a jazz song, broadcast around the world on vampire radio. (A montage of listeners around the world includes a vampire couple in their cosy coffin-for-two.) From now on, vampires everywhere will be able to enjoy beach holidays.

Coda, a year or so later. Pepe is playing at an open-air bar; Lola dandles their first-born on her knee. The little tyke looks out at us, and grins. He has fangs.

PAR†Y ON, UNDEAD DUDES;
OR, DRACULA MEE†S PE†ER PAN

The poster for *The Lost Boys* (1987, directed by Joel Schumacher) had a memorable catchline: 'Sleep all day. Party all night. Never grow old. Never die. It's fun to be a vampire'. And that pretty much sums it up. Purists tend to despise this film; dabblers tend to think it's really cool, dude. This time, I'm with the purists; though there are, to be scrupulously fair, some decent touches here and there (the special effects are more than adequate, and there is a nice element of mythology-tinkering: the vampire boys eschew coffins, and hang upside down from a cave roof to sleep, as if they were real-life bats). But it is something of a mess, and never – unlike, say, *Innocent Blood* – finds the right balance between sophomoric comedy and chills.

Plot: a couple of teenage boys are moved to 'Santa Clara', a coastal town in California, after their mother (Dianne Wiest) divorces. Though the place seems harmless enough on the surface, signs declare it a 'murder capital'. We soon discover why. The young lads are sucked in by the cheesy glamour of the local biker gang (the leader is played by Kiefer Sutherland), whose nocturnal ways prove to have the usual cause; then, with the help of their grandpa and a couple of know-all pubescent kids who run a comic book store, and moonlight as Van

Helsings – and appear to have wandered in from another movie altogether – they fight back. If this sounds like a lot of fun, it isn't.

A much sounder choice is a near-contemporary production, *Near Dark* (see below).

THE FAMILY THAT PREYS TOGETHER

Near Dark (1987, directed and co-written by the versatile and seldom disappointing action specialist Kathryn Bigelow). Bigelow's film has worn well with the years and is highly regarded in some discerning circles. (The British director Danny Boyle recently named it one of his top five films, alongside *Apocalypse Now*.) One of its unusual touches is that its informal 'family' of vampires are a long way indeed from the snooty, Old European Counts and Grafs of Romantic and Hollywood convention alike. In fact, the film is set in the American south-west, and the vampires are a bunch of uncouth hillbillies and rednecks (pun not originally intended by me, though it doubtless occurred to Ms Bigelow and company). An innocent young farm hand, Caleb, comes across a tomboyish teenage girl, Mae, who bites him after he rather too forcefully demands a kiss. Almost at once, he begins to develop vampire symptoms, stumbling around in nauseated agony when the sun rises, but is reluctant to kill, even to ease the symptoms of his affliction, which grow worse and worse. Meanwhile, his new associates are not too sure that they want this newcomer on board their bus.

Eventually, Caleb manages to win their acceptance by saving them from a police raid, but just as he is starting to settle into this odd new family, his father comes and rescues him, then administers a blood transfusion in the hope of flushing away the vampire contaminants. It works! (Probably for the first time in movie history.) Mae pines for Caleb, and wants him back; the gang attacks his house and kidnaps his younger sister Sarah. Shifting allegiances, Mae rescues Sarah and, after accepting a transfusion from Caleb's father, appears to revert to human form. A happy ending? Probably not: Mae adored being a vampire, since she was in love with the prospect of immortality. Bigelow's film is finely shot and tautly edited, gruesome fight scenes giving place to awe-inducing vistas of the south-western night skies.

BATS IN THE BELFRY

Vampire's Kiss (1989, directed by Robert Bierman) is a very unusual movie – half harrowing psychodrama, half over-the-top black comedy – starring Nicolas Cage as Peter, a high-flying and more than mildly unpleasant New York literary agent who, having been bitten by a bat (and, later, or so it seems, by a female vampire), starts to show more and more symptoms of vampirism – sensitivity to daylight and so on. His nasty ways grow increasingly obnoxious, as if being an arrogant, hysterical bully were one of the classic traits of vampirism. He dumps his long-suffering girlfriend, browbeats a naive young Hispanic woman who works at his agency, and experiences uncontrollable fits of anger at his therapist's and elsewhere.

Shrewder viewers will by now have picked up on the fact that all the 'supernatural' sequences we have witnessed are in fact taking place only inside Peter's head, and that what we are watching is a man spiralling down into mania. Eventually, Peter's conviction that he has become a vampire reaches a grotesque conclusion. After violently raping his secretary, he sets off on a hunting spree, equipped with a three-dollar pair of plastic fangs. Lurking around night spots with his eyes popping in broad imitation of Max Shreck (we see a couple of sequences from *Nosferatu* on Peter's television), Peter ultimately kills a young woman in a disco. He has his comeuppance, however, in a manner which any Hammer fan could foresee. Well worth checking out as a period satire, the film also includes one of the most shudder-inducing moments in all cinema: Cage picks up a huge, obviously real cockroach, shoves it in his mouth and chews. (The camera pans away before he swallows, but, even so . . . ick.)

COSA NOSFERATU: THE VAMPIRE AS MAFIOSO

Innocent Blood (1993, directed by John Landis, who also made the much better-known *An American Werewolf in London*) is one of the few mainstream vampire films with genuinely funny moments. Anne Parillaud stars as Marie, a seductive she-vampire with an unexplained French accent, on the loose in Pittsburgh, where she preys exclusively on criminals – to be exact, on members of the local Mafia. (Italian food, as she thinks of them.) A local cop (Anthony LaPaglia), working undercover until his identity is revealed by the press, comes into conflict with her but, eventually, falls for her undead charms. Connoisseurs of wholly gratuitous nudity will relish the opening sequence, in which Marie wanders starkers around her candlelit apartment for no obvious dramatic reason.

The plot takes a gruesome turn when the local gang boss, torn apart by Marie and left for dead, rises up on his morgue slab and goes home to run business as usual. Gradually, and to his delight, the capo realises that he is now bullet-proof, knife-proof . . . in short, indestructible. He begins systematically to 'turn' his henchman into a vampire criminal army, thus giving a new meaning to the Mob slang term 'a made man'. He seems unstoppable, until Marie joins forces with her policeman lover and . . . stops him. Not often screened these days, *Innocent Blood* is a lively and inventive mixture of thriller and comedy, which – a Landis trademark – makes liberal use of juxtaposing its action with the action of old films glimpsed on television sets: here, both Christopher Lee (from the final sequence of *Horror of Dracula*) and Bela Lugosi (the 'children of the night' sequence).

THE GODFATHER OF ALL VAMPIRES: COPPOLA
REVIVES STOKER

The most expensive and lavishly publicized vampire film to date, *Bram Stoker's Dracula* – also known by the even more cumbersome title *Francis Ford Coppola's Bram Stoker's Dracula*, which is surely one possessive too far – was released in 1992 to a very healthy box office (it remains the fourth most profitable vampire movie of the last three decades; see above) and generally respectful reviews. Purists disliked it. To say the least. 'A major disappointment' – David J. Skal, *V is for Vampire*; 'A wretched movie truly deserving of everyone's contempt' – Lyndon W. Joslin, *Count Dracula Goes to the Movies*. They had good reason, and most of the standard objections to Coppola's creation are hard if not impossible to dispute. I am perverse enough to find it hugely enjoyable, but let us first consider the case for the prosecution.

The initial complaint is also the most damaging: by calling the movie *Bram Stoker's Dracula*, the producers were implicitly promising a return to the true source, and much of the attendant publicity innocently or ignorantly backed up that boast. Now, it is certainly true that Coppola's *Dracula* – based on a screenplay by James V. Hart – does jump back over the various conflations of character, warpings of geography and assorted additional tinkerings which marked every major reworking of the tale from Murnau to Hammer. The film restores Stoker's fundamental three-part structure of Transylvania/England/Transylvania, ignored by all predecessors. Coppola also brings back the Texan character Quincey P. Morris; firmly separates the characters of Mina and Lucy, often swapped around or conflated; makes great erotic play with the three 'Brides of Dracula', generally unseen in this context since their rather chaste appearance in the Browning film (though the 1977 BBC version also included the trio, not very memorably). Above all, Coppola returns to Stoker's device of documentary collage – Seward's recordings, Mina's typewriter journal, Harker's letters. So far, so accurate.

What really makes purists howl is the film's prologue, and the damage it inflicts on everything that follows. To put it simply, this *Dracula* has become a love story, with a reincarnation theme. Buying into the Van Helsing theory that Dracula is none other than Vlad the Impaler, the film begins in 1462, and shows Vlad's forces brutally repelling the Turk. But a treacherous rumour reaches Vlad's beautiful young wife Elisabeta, so that she believes her gallant husband is dead, and in her despair jumps to her death from the turrets of Castle Dracula. When Vlad returns, he is so horrified and enraged by this reward for having defended Christendom that he rejects God and stabs the giant crucifix in his chapel, which gushes with supernatural blood. This, then, is his birth as a vampire (Stoker hints at other origins). It also explains the principal reason, usually left untroubled in earlier adaptations, for why he should be so keen to come to England. The answer: Mina is the nineteenth-century avatar of his wife's spirit; he has come to reclaim his young bride.

Stoker purists are already queuing at the box office, demanding their money back. But is it really such a bad conceit? Very few people raised objections to the 'reincarnated love' theme when it was used in the 1973 Dan Curtis adaptation of *Dracula* with Jack Palance (see p.80, 'Who Was the Real Dracula?'), or in *Blacula*, or *Love at First Bite* . . . or, come to that, in the Universal Pictures movie of *The Mummy*, which is probably the deep inspiration for all of them. But the purists' objections to Coppola's creation do not stop there. They say that the film's acting is awful; the interpretations of character either muddled or just plain wrong (in this film, Lucy is an overtly sexy gal from the kick-off; when she becomes even sexier after the vampire's kiss, it hardly comes as a mild surprise, let alone a shock); and that most of the American actors speak with embarrassingly fake English accents, while the British actors (Gary Oldman as Dracula, Anthony Hopkins as Van Helsing) adopt corny 'continental' accents.

Agreed, agreed, agreed. But what has not been mentioned so far is the film's single most striking facet: its visual design, its costumes, its camera effects. Sceptics find all of these over-ripe, garish, vulgar; believers think they can be ravishing. Eiko Ishioka deservedly won the Academy Award for best costumes, and they truly are exceptional creations, from the blazing red man-wolf carapace of armour worn by Vlad in the opening scene, to the lizard-like ruffs of Lucy's gown, to the reworking of Dracula's rampant-dragon coat of arms into a handle for his cane. Almost every frame of the film could have come from a supernatural edition of *Vogue*. And then there are the camera effects. In an age, the early 1990s, already beginning to be glutted to repletion by computer wizardry, Coppola chose to revive the late-1890s, Méliès-style trickery of the silent cinema – superimpositions, painted mattes and, in the case of the opening battles between Christians and Muslims, a technology far more ancient than the cinema: shadow puppets, like the wayang theatre of South-East Asia.

Coppola's movie also underlines, as very few films have ever tried (there is a creditable attempt in the first Hammer *Dracula*), Stoker's dramatic juxtapositions of state-of-the-art Victorian English technology and the darkness of the late Middle Ages. There are blood transfusions, recording technologies, and even – a case of content inspired by style – the kinematograph, which is where Mina and Dracula go on their first 'date'. But the director also draws deeply on the literary and artistic culture of the 1890s as well as its sciences, so that the film is, to borrow a phrase, a kind of 'breviary of the Decadence', saturated with references to Symbolist art, drugs, the 'Green Fairy' of absinthe (is the whole tale a kind of drugged dream?), *femmes fatales*, occultism and fashionable Orientalism (we see Lucy and Mina peeping at the Kama Sutra – and perhaps recall that the translator of the book, Richard Burton, was one of Stoker's possible models for Dracula). There is also at least one direct visual reference to Murnau's film, when the Count, dressed in a Klimt-inspired robe, swings up from his coffin.

Does any of this compensate for, say, Keanu Reeves's Dick Van Dyke English or his plank-like performance as Harker? Well, yes, I think it more than compensates; and I also believe that Coppola's film is one of the most unflaggingly entertaining and inventive of all vampire films. Oh: and Hopkins is sly, funny, and charismatic as Van Helsing. Those who say that he should have been given the title role are probably right, in some ways.

Everyone, by the way, should read Kim Newman's brilliant short story in the *Anno Dracula* sequence, 'Coppola's Dracula', which has the American director shooting an ambitious, troubled *Apocalypse Now*-style epic in Wallachia.

SANG SUR MES DENTS:
KIM NEWMAN'S ANNO DRACULA SERIES

If the literary world paid more attention to genre fiction, Kim Newman would be recognized as one of Britain's most gifted, ambitious and erudite novelists; and the *Anno Dracula* series as a dark jewel in the national literary crown. To date, this extraordinary extended work runs to three full-length novels:

✝ *Anno Dracula* (1992).

✝ *The Bloody Red Baron* (1995).

✝ *Dracula Cha Cha Cha* (1998; also known as *Judgment of Tears*).

One novella:

✝ *Andy Warhol's Dracula* (2000).

And some short stories from the same alternative universe – 'Coppola's Dracula', 'Castle in the Desert', 'The Other Side of Midnight' (the Orson Welles Dracula story), 'A Concert for Transylvania', 'Who Dares Wins' and 'You Are the Wind Beneath My Wings'. Kim Newman says that he plans to integrate all of these short stories into a much longer narrative with the working title of *Johnny Alucard*.

The earliest glimmering of this wonderfully entertaining saga was a footnote to a long essay Newman wrote when he was an undergraduate, in 1978. His theme was the 'invasion' motif in late nineteenth-century fiction – *The War of the Worlds*, *The Battle of Dorking* and so on. Newman noted the implied presence of this theme in *Dracula*, and he speculated on how interesting it would be to imagine a world in which the Count's 'invasion' had succeeded. A decade and a half later, this speculation flowered into *Anno Dracula*.

Newman's premise is that Dracula's one-vampire invasion succeeded; he killed Van Helsing, married Queen Victoria, and overthrew the traditional class system: now it is the undead who are the top dogs, and the living – 'warm' – population who have to struggle to survive. Some warm citizens affect vampiric appearances, and try to pass for undead; others, still more ambitious, take the bite and climb the social ladder. Unflaggingly ingenious, the novel is crammed with late Victorians, both real-life and fictional, from Gilbert and Sullivan to Jack the Ripper (who turns out to be Dracula's enemy Dr Seward). The sequels are, if anything, even more ingenious. *The Bloody Red Baron* is set in 1918, at the climax of the war. Graf von Dracula, now expelled from Britain, is supreme commander of the combined armed forces of Germany and the Austro-Hungarian Empire; Dracula's former ally, Lord Ruthven, is Prime Minister. The supporting cast includes Edgar Allan Poe, brought back from the dead. *Dracula Cha Cha Cha* is set in Rome in 1959 – the period of *La Dolce Vita*: Dracula is set to marry a princess, but the Eternal City is also in a state of panic, since a serial staker called the Crimson Executioner is destroying the cream of vampire society. Enter an undead British secret agent, with a license to kill: the name is Bond. Hamish Bond . . .

Enough. Read them and relish.

DESIGNER SHROUDS AND REAL BLOODY MARYS:
THE VAMPIRE AS YUPPIE

The only recent vampire fiction to rival Kim Newman's for wit and narrative brio is a very different kind of novel, Anne Billson's *Suckers* (1993), which won her a place on the *Granta* magazine list of best British writers under forty. One of the book's fans, Salman Rushdie, pronounced it a satire, and this verdict became widely repeated – a mixed blessing, as the author's aims were only partly satirical. *Suckers* is also a novel of jaded, disenchanted love; an exercise in that traditional theme of horror fiction, the surprise return of the supposedly defeated evil; and even, by its bleak finale, a vision of apocalypse.

The heroine and narrator, Dora – an unexpectedly likeable presence, for all that her hobbies include staying up all night writing hate mail to an otherwise blameless woman who once annoyed her – becomes uneasily aware that the discreet but rapid rise of a new multinational corporation might have something to do with a nasty episode from her student days; an episode which ended with her hacking up the body of a female vampire and disposing of the bits and pieces all over town. She also starts to realize that all the chic, pale-faced young men and women in black clothes who now seem to be running London may be drinking something a touch more wicked than vodka and tomato juice. The most unforgettable scene has Dora trapped in a select vampire bar, frightened out of her wits and trying to look undead herself. Then her period starts . . .

It all ends with something called *Rotnacht*; and very nasty it is, too. Highly recommended.

Meanwhile, Anne Billson has been kind enough to donate a list of the ten vampire films she most highly recommends:

✝ *Dracula's Daughter* (1936).

✝ *The Kiss of the Vampire* (1963).

✝ *I Tre volti della paura*, aka *Black Sabbath* (1963).

✝ *Dracula, Prince of Darkness* (1966).

✝ *Dance of the Vampires* (1967).

✝ *Daughters of Darkness* aka *Les Lèvres rouges* (1971).

✝ *Martin* (1977).

✝ *Salem's Lot* (1979).

✝ *Mr Vampire*, aka *Geung si sin sang* (1985).

✝ *Near Dark* (1987).

✝ *Let the Right One In* (2008).

CHILLI CON CARNAGE: MEXICAN VAMPIRES

Cronos (1993, directed by Guillermo del Toro) was the breakthrough film of the young Mexican director. It enjoyed considerable international success, both critically (it took the Critic's Week Award at Cannes, and won nine Mexican Academy Awards) and commercially. The nature of del Toro's vampire is unique: it is an antique wind-up toy, small enough to hold in the palm of the hand, and somewhat resembling a cross between a scarab and a scorpion, which was made by a sixteenth-century alchemist, in quest of eternal life. (Del Toro's subsequent films have shown that he has a penchant for this kind of clockwork universe.) Lurking inside the clockwork is a deathless parasite, the bite of which can indeed confer immortality. At a price; a very familiar price. Anyone bitten will develop a dreadful aversion to sunlight, and a thirst for human blood . . . Some critics saw the film as a parable of US capitalism, leeching on Latin nations; maybe, but the film's appeal was largely due to its fluent storytelling and touches of visual poetry.

Del Toro's subsequent career has been an interesting combination of art-house works (*The Devil's Backbone, Pan's Labyrinth*) and more conventional multiplex fodder (*Hellboy, Hellboy II*). To date, his only other excursion into vampire territory on screen has been *Blade II* (see below); but he is reported to have signed a contract to co-write three vampire novels with a contemporary setting.

FANGED ANGST: EXISTENTIAL VAMPIRES

Fans of more orthodox vampire fodder usually find Michael Almereyda's *Nadja* (1994) boring, pretentious and confused. They're not being altogether philistine about this, as the comedian Bill Bailey pointed out when he introduced a screening of the film on British television. But there are many things to enjoy in this poverty-row production shot almost wholly in black and white, and partly on a cheap toy camera. (Almereyda calls the process 'Pixelvision'.) If some of it is murky and confused, some of it is also unexpectedly beautiful. It stars Elina Löwensohn as 'Nadja' (the obvious allusion to André Breton's autobiographical novel of that name is never explained), an achingly lovely New York demi-mondaine who turns out to be Dracula's daughter. Indeed, a good deal of the plot is based quite closely on *Dracula's Daughter*, the 1936 Universal film.

Here, the young vampiress is a modern-day bohemian, who drifts around late-night bars in New York, chain-smoking, guzzling coffee and soliloquizing, usually in an anhedonic monotone. Things drift along until she suddenly has the premonition that her father is finally dead – staked by Van Helsing (Peter Fonda, in a weird and overblown performance). Accompanied by her man Renfield, she goes to the morgue and declares to the attendant (played by David Lynch, who was one of the producers), 'We have come for the body of Count Voivoda Arminis Ceaucescu Dracula,' – a line which makes *Najda* the first American vampire film to pick up on the frequent identification of Romania's late dictator with the Lord of the Undead. After this, things grow considerably more complex, and considerably more Sapphic.

HOOKED: VAMPIRES AS (BLOODY OBVIOUS) METAPHOR

Many vampire films had played with the metaphor of vampirism as drug addiction; in the very first Hammer *Dracula* film, for instance, Van

Helsing (Peter Cushing) has a literate digression on the similarity of the two altered states. It was not until Abel Ferrara's *The Addiction* (1995), though, that anyone saw fit to make the connection quite so glaring, and to convert creeping subtext into brazen main text. (Seldom a good idea.) This is a fair indication of what the film as a whole is like: as subtle as a wooden stake to the heart, and about as enjoyable.

Some otherwise reliable critics have admired this plodding, studiedly nasty work, possibly for its ostentatious nihilism. It begins with the heroine, a philosophy graduate student at NYU, name of Kathleen (Lili Taylor – actually very good, given the thankless nature of her role), looking at photographs of concentration camp victims: soul-rending sights that we are not spared, and which make the rest of the proceedings seem still more meretricious. Kathleen is attacked on the street by a female vampire (Annabella Sciorra) and, well, you can imagine most of the rest, except possibly Christopher Walken's cameo as her vampire tutor.

RESERVOIR BATS;
OR, QUENTIN TARANTINO DOES VAMPIRES

From Dusk Till Dawn (1996, directed by Robert Rodriguez, from the screenplay by Quentin Tarentino). A decade and more on, the cat, or bat, is now thoroughly out of the bag about this film's major plot twist – the least predictable of any Hollywood film since *Psycho*, or perhaps ever – so that nowadays it is increasingly hard to have the fun of sneaking a look at the neophyte sitting next to you when the movie's genre abruptly skips rails and they squeak with shock. (If you don't wish to know the precise nature of that twist just yet, please skip the following paragraphs and rent the DVD.) For about the first two-thirds of its running time, *From Dusk Till Dawn* appears to be a straightforwardly brutal, occasionally darkly comic crime thriller. The Gecko brothers, a brace of black-suited escaped convicts, are on the run from the Texas Rangers and the FBI, having just slaughtered a number of policemen and civilians in a messy bank raid. As the film begins, they jack up their death toll a few more points by killing some innocents in a highway liquor store, and then blowing it up. We swiftly learn that the older brother Seth (George Clooney), though utterly ruthless, is a professional criminal and not without a hint of personal charm; his younger brother Richie (Tarantino) is dim-witted, delusional and psychopathic. Left alone for a couple of hours to mind their first kidnap victim, a matronly bank employee, he soon rapes and kills her.

The police net is closing in, and the Geckos need to make it across the border into Mexico, so they take fresh hostages: Jacob, a quietly spoken, recently lapsed minister (Harvey Keitel) and his two teenage children, Kate (Juliet Lewis) and Scott (Ernest Liu). With the daughter held at gunpoint in the bathroom of their RV, the minister manages to talk them past the border patrol and into the safety of Mexico, where the Geckos have an appointment with a local gang boss. They pull into the agreed rendezvous point – an all-night bar ('Open from dusk till dawn') which rejoices in the name of the Titty Twister. This proves to be a swinish dive, where truckers and bikers beat each other senseless, topless dancing girls preen and tease, and a mangy bar band grinds out rock music. Seth likes it a lot, and likes it all the more when an exotic dancer, Santanico Pandemonium (Salma Hayek), comes and struts her stuff with a giant, pale yellow snake. Then trouble begins to brew. One of the club's bouncers comes in, complaining that Seth has broken his wrist (true). There's a scuffle . . . and then hell breaks loose.

Literally. In a twinkling, Santanico morphs into a fanged monster; then all the other bar employees instantly spout their own fangs, claws, wings and so on. They are all vampires! The hordes of undead tear into the living – as is obviously their standard policy – and blood and guts fly in all directions. But some of the living are not so easily dispatched, and, with the Gecko brothers leading the fight, quite a few of the vampires are soon safely pinned down and staked. Respite is brief, since the newly bitten humans start coming back to life as vampires, too. Seth gives Jacob a pep talk, and the disillusioned minister regains at least enough of his faith to start turning tap water into holy water, which acts on vampire flesh like strong acid.

Eventually, only Seth and Kate are left alive, holding a swarm of bat-like vampires at bay . . . when shafts of light, from the bullet holes in the wall, start to blaze into the depths of the evil joint. Seth and Kate run to the doors, and a flood of dawn light, reflected into countless shafts by a glitter ball, sees off the final attacking brutes. Seth makes a deal with the Mexican gang boss; he and Kate drive off into the distance and their respective futures. The film's final, panoramic shot pulls back and upwards to reveal that the vampire bar stands on the edge of a giant quarry, littered with abandoned vehicles; and that it is, in fact, no more than a modern façade at the summit of an enormous, ziggurat-like structure. The implication is plain – this has been a place of supernatural evil since pre-Colombian times.

Thanks partly to Tarantino's still-fashionable standing at the time of release, the film was successful enough to spawn two sequels, with Tarantino and Rodriguez in the roles of executive producers, but writing and direction in the hands of others.

From Dusk Till Dawn 2: Texas Blood Money (1999, directed and co-written by Scott Spiegel). This is a dreary and mainly negligible yarn, with almost no connection to the original save for a scene in the Titty Twister. It was shot in South Africa on a low budget (about $5 million) and went straight to video. Briefly: a convict, Luther, breaks out of jail and contacts his old crony Buck to round up a new gang for a bank job. Buck assembles the gang, and they hole up for a while in a seedy motel, El Coyote. Meanwhile, en route to the rendezvous, Luther hits and apparently kills a bat – actually a vampire. He walks from his broken car to the nearest bar – yes, that one – and is offered a ride by

Razor Eddie. But when Razor Eddie finds out about the accident, he bites and turns Luther.

Meanwhile, the gang are whiling away their time watching porn movies on cable, or, in the case of Jesus, having sex with a local floozie. Luther, now in full vampire mode, kills and turns the floozie in a bloody scene that rather heavy-handedly alludes to the shower scene in *Psycho*. Then the gang set off to rob a bank, but their efforts are somewhat hindered by divided ambitions: the vamps, caring more for blood than lucre, keep biting and turning everybody in sight. Everything culminates in a massive shoot-out with a SWAT team, some of it set during a solar eclipse which allows the vampires briefly to function in daylight. At the end of the action, only Buck and his old nemesis Sheriff Otis are left standing.

From Dusk Till Dawn 3: The Hangman's Daughter (2000, directed by P. J. Pesce). In defiance of the usual law of cultural entropy, which holds that each subsequent sequel of a franchise grows weaker and weaker, the third and (presumably) final part of the *DTD* trilogy has a number of fresh and entertaining touches. Shot and paced much like a spaghetti western, *From Dusk Till Dawn 3* is, strictly speaking, a prequel rather than a sequel – a period piece, which incorporates the true-life story of the American writer Ambrose Bierce, and his mysterious disappearance in Mexico on the eve of the First World War. (Bierce's vanishing is also the subject of, among other works, Carlos Fuentes's novel *The Old Gringo*.) The film begins with Bierce (played by Michael Parks) witnessing the eleventh-hour – indeed, virtually the twelfth-hour – escape of an outlaw, Johnny Madrid, from the gallows. Madrid runs off with the hangman's daughter, Esmerelda (Ara Celi). Closely pursued by the law, Madrid manages to reunite his old posse of villains, and they hold up a stagecoach, in the mistaken belief that it contains a cache of gold bullion.

On board the coach are Bierce, who explains that he is off to meet

Zapata (this would place the action of the film either in 1913 or in 1914, the latter date being the one usually given for Bierce's presumed death); and a married couple who are, they say, planning to bring the Bible to remote areas – though the husband is not all that he seems. Night falls, and everyone takes shelter in the nearest available refuge – a large and lavish whorehouse (clearly, to the informed viewer, an earlier version of the Titty Twister). The vampires show their fangs, and we learn that Esmerelda is actually a half-human vampire princess, Santanico Pandemonium – the part played by Salma Hayek in the first movie. After a long night of bloodshed, once again only two humans are left alive, Bierce and Madrid. A final shot of the reverse side of the whorehouse once again shows the Aztec-like structure we witnessed in the very first film.

Curious afterthought: Ambrose Bierce himself wrote some classic vampire stories.

DIME-STORE DRACULAS, ACT TWO: BLADE

Already well known to readers of Marvel comics, the character of Blade reached a much wider audience in 1998, with the release of a film version of his adventures starring Wesley Snipes. Blade is that once-paradoxical, now-routine thing, a vampire superhero; to date, the most famous of his kind. (He is also, for the time being, the most famous black vampire, though the films do not draw particular attention to his ethnicity, the only conspicuous nod to African-American culture in the series being its lavish use of bone-shakingly loud rap music on the soundtrack.) Strictly speaking, Blade is a sort of vampire hybrid, a Ninja-like swordsman and 'Day Walker', who owes his half-and-half condition to the fact that his mother was bitten when pregnant with him. Unlike his near-kindred, Blade is able to walk in daylight without harm; he is also able to soothe, if not entirely satisfy, his raging thirst for blood with an artificial serum, though there is the constant threat that he may one day find this substitute too pallid, and return to vampire type.

The plots of the *Blade* films are complex and not a particularly important component of their appeal. A brief survey of the film trilogy:

Blade (1998, directed by Stephen Norrington). We first encounter Blade when he intervenes in an ingeniously nasty atrocity: naive human beings have been lured into a rave club – hidden behind a giant abattoir – by hungry undead. Suddenly, blood gushes from the sprinkler system and carnage begins. (In its way, this is quite well done.) Enter Blade, angry as hell, who wipes out all of the vampires save one. After this arresting set piece, the narrative gives way to a larger scheme. The villain of the piece, Deacon Frost (played by Stephen Dorff), is an upstart young vampire who wants the species to come out from the shadows and wage open war. His deeper plan is to awaken an ancient vampire god, La Magra, using the blood of vampire elders. With the help of the series' Van Helsing figure, Abraham (*sic*) Whistler (Kris Kristofferson, long-haired and curmudgeonly), Blade foils and destroys Frost. Whistler appears to have died.

Blade II (2002, directed by Guillermo del Toro). Blade has to join forces with his previous enemies, the Bloodpack, to defeat a new strain of super-vampires known as the Reapers. Whistler is brought back from the dead. Blade wins.

Blade Trinity (2006, directed by David S. Goyer, the series' screenwriter). This instalment is notable in plot terms for bringing back Dracula – 'Drake', he is called here – who has been buried somewhere in the Syrian desert. (At one point Drake refers dismissively to 'the fable by Stoker'.) A new vampire posse headed by Danica Talos (Parker Posey) try to prevent Blade from messing with their schemes by framing him for a murder, thus putting the FBI on his trail. Blade teams up with a new set of human vampire hunters. Among the film's better grace notes: a vampire Pomeranian with gigantic jaws; and the repeated suggestion that, in this world, Esperanto is widely spoken alongside English.

There was a short-lived television spin-off in 2006, with Sticky Fingaz in the title role. At the time of writing, there are rumours that, if Snipes can settle his differences with the studio and a few other difficulties (he is in prison for tax evasion), a *Blade 4* may go into production. Meanwhile, Blade's adventures continue in a series of comics.

VAMPIRES AMONG †HE CHEERLEADERS: ON †HE GENIUS OF BUFFY, †HE VAMPIRE SLAYER

The Best of all Vampire Television?

Thanks in part to the inspired bathos of the title – matched in recent times only by an avant-garde poem about cheerleaders entitled *Debbie: An Epic* – almost everyone with a pulse and ready access to the mass media has at least heard of this strange and dangerously addictive series. (Imagine how much less amusing it would all have seemed with a classic girl's name: *Caroline, the Vampire Slayer; Laura, the Vampire Slayer* . . .) Far fewer people have ever watched it often; and fewer still have followed it through all seven series. But, as has been observed in the many, many critical studies of the phenomenon, the relatively modest *Buffy* has lodged itself in popular culture every bit as firmly as blockbusters like *Star Wars*, and, for true fans of the series, its emotional potency exceeds just about anything that American television has ever produced.

For those who have yet to catch the *Buffy* bug, this degree of adulation can only seem baffling. The thing, after all, is at heart a kiddie show, set in a suburban high school, aimed mainly at teenagers and pre-teens, and preoccupied (in its realist mode) with dating, nice clothes, popularity, homework and the culture-clashes of nerds and jocks. In its non-realist mode, it is just downright silly. Its main premise is that the youthful heroine, a petite blonde name of Buffy Summers, is both fated for all eternity to slay vampires, and blessed with all the powers she needs to carry out that grim task (immense strength, dazzling acrobatic skills, mastery of martial arts). She is kept busy, since her home town of Sunnydale is sited on a kind of inter-dimensional portal, the Hellmouth, through which all the ghouls and dark forces of the universe can pass freely into our world. Buffy spends her days at school, and her nights putting stakes into the hearts of vampires, each of which obligingly explodes into a cloud of dust. Broadly speaking, each episode displays a new Demon of the Week, neatly dispatched in time for the final credits.

So why should anyone much over the age of fifteen pay any attention to this affable tosh? The quickest answers both require only two words: either (a) 'the writing', or (b) 'Joss Whedon'. Since Whedon, a third-generation showbiz kid born in 1964, wrote the original outline for the whole series, plus its various spin-offs, and scripted the majority of its most celebrated episodes, these answers are very nearly synonymous. As Anne Billson points out in her excellent BFI monograph on the series, Whedon increasingly began to act towards the world of *Buffy* – the 'Buffyverse', in fanspeak – as a capricious, restlessly inventive God might treat his Creation. Let's see, what shall we do with it next . . . ?

Within the constraints of its prime-time format, Whedon somehow found the freedom to dramatize material that was far darker and more weird than mainstream television can usually encompass; he went off on flights of wit and fancy comparable, at their best, to anything in *The Simpsons*. Perhaps the most famous episode of the show – 'Once More, With Feeling' – is staged almost entirely as a Technicolor musical comedy, and it's a brilliantly observed pastiche of American show tunes across the decades, from the thirties and forties to the age of the Power Ballad, with cleverly rhyming lyrics that might have made Lorenz Hart smile.

Whedon also devised an episode, 'Hush', in which all the characters are robbed of their powers of speech by some truly creepy demons called the Gentlemen, so that a good two-thirds of the action was conducted without dialogue. There was another which borrowed the central conceit of *It's a Wonderful Life*, and showed what Sunnydale would have been like had Buffy not appeared; another which hops between two alternative realities, and leaves open the possibility that the Buffy we have come to know over several years is actually the inmate of a mental hospital, and all her screen adventures no more than a consoling fantasy world. (Which, in another sense, they obviously are.)

All of which can be as enjoyable as it is unusual. Far from requiring the viewer to turn off all higher mental functions for forty-odd minutes, the show increasingly rewards sharp ears, keen eyes and a reasonably ample range of cultural awareness. Finally, though, the cleverness of the show is less telling than its power to move audiences deeply, since Whedon has always maintained that, however unrealistic the show might become in its fooling around with magic and the supernatural, it should always remain as realistic as possible at the level of emotions. As Anne Billson rightly points out, Buffy, the character, would soon grow boring if she were merely an indestructible Superchick; but her physical strength is matched by an emotional vulnerability consistent with the fact that she is also just a teenager, worried about boys and school and her mother (who, in a late episode that some viewers found much too harrowing, dies from a brain tumour).

Perhaps most important of all: Buffy is a great *female* action hero. At last, little (and not so little) girls have their own counterpart of Superman, or Indiana Jones, or James Bond, or Sherlock Holmes as fodder for the exciting daydreams that every growing child needs. Hardly surprising that most feminists who have checked the show out sooner or later end up giving a big thumbs-up to Mr Whedon and all his works. Buffy, to adapt an Americanism, kicks rump.

Some Aspects of the Buffyverse

Buffy has its unlikely origins in a poorly executed, low-budget (about $7 million), not conspicuously successful feature film, released in 1992. It was directed by a woman, Fran Rubel Kuzui, but the credit to watch was the male screenwriter's (Joss Whedon; see above). Buffy, who in the film was meant to be eighteen, was played by Kirsty Swanson, then in her twenties. Buffy's mentor figure or Watcher was played by Donald Sutherland. It was all a bit of a mess, neither funny enough nor spooky enough, and left Whedon dissatisfied, feeling that most of the promise had been squandered. His fundamental idea was a very simple one. Just about every horror film of recent years had featured a fragile, often simple-minded blonde girl who wanders into a dark house or down a dark alley and is duly slaughtered. But what, Whedon asked himself, if that girl refused to let herself be stabbed, axed, clubbed or bitten? What if she fought back, and proved to be the heroine?

He had his chance for reparations when Warner Brothers commissioned twelve episodes of *Buffy* as a mid-season replacement for a now-forgotten soap called *Savannah*. This time, he made sure it was done right. *Buffy* went on to run for seven series, broadcast from 1997 to 2003; there were 144 episodes (most of them conceived as Demon of the Week stories, though each one contributed to larger story arcs and character development, which amounts to 96 hours of broadcasting or about 64 average-length feature films; it also generated a major spin-off series, *Angel*, on which more below). One implication of these statistics: it needs a book, or several books, to provide even a passably informative account of all the characters, narratives, themes and conceits that filled all those hours. But one can convey at least something of the series' unique qualities by looking at a few of the major characters – particularly the quartet Whedon has called the 'Core Four': Buffy, Giles, Willow and Xander.

Buffy (Sarah Michelle Gellar). The Slayer. 'In every generation there is a Chosen One. She alone will stand against the Vampires . . . She is the Slayer.' As the series begins, Buffy is a newcomer to Sunnydale High, and just sixteen years old (having magically lost two years since the film version, though characters sometimes refer to her having burned down her previous high school – the climactic sequence of the movie). She grows up in approximately real time across the seven series, moving on to college; has many flirtations and three major affairs, notably with a supernatural chap called Angel, who is a 241-year-old vampire under a vindictive gypsy curse; dies twice; loses her mother; has financial difficulties, takes on blue-collar jobs; and averts the End of the World, usually about once per series.

Giles (Anthony Head; or, as the credits call him, Anthony Stewart Head). The Watcher: in other words, the Van Helsing of the Buffyverse. The only adult central character. In his mid-forties or thereabouts, handsome in a tweedy kind of way, and every casting director's idea of a classic, stuffy Englishman, though a sympathetic character nonetheless (and played with many a sly and comic touch by Head, who is perfect in the role).

Willow (Alyson Hannigan). Buffy's friend, and, of the Core Four, the character who undergoes the most radical changes, from a rather drippy outsider, to a dabbler in Wicca, to a full-blown spell-casting witch (she becomes a lesbian at roughly the same time, having broken up with her boyfriend Oz, a werewolf), to a kind of 'magick addict', to a full-blown villain with the usual apocalyptic ambitions.

Xander (Nicholas Brandon). The Everyman character, slightly gauche, self-deprecating and with a rather wobbly and unsuccessful love life; he becomes engaged to a former demon called Anya, but runs out on their marriage. He is usually the only (human) boy member of Buffy's vampire-busting posse – they call themselves the Scooby Gang or the Scoobies, in homage to the cartoon series about a ghost-busting dog. He is said to be the character with whom Whedon most identifies.

There are dozens of other notable characters, including the stroppy, (eventually) good vampire Spike (James Marsters), who in one episode mixes Weetabix in his mug of plasma to lend it body, and in his warm-blooded days was an appallingly talentless Victorian poet. Spike has a huge fan base, is the star of his own comics series, and may yet be the subject of a feature film (see below). And there are hundreds of supporting characters, villains and monsters . . . including none other than Dracula himself, in the episode 'Buffy vs. Dracula'. Across its 144 instalments, *Buffy* created – as all satisfying fantasies should – an entire, densely populated world, full of texture and, at times, depth. Sample a few of the better episodes with an open mind, and you may surprised at how thoroughly it draws you in.

PS. The title track to *Buffy* is performed by a band called Nerf Herder. Looks like an anagram, but in fact is an allusion to a line in *The Empire Strikes Back*: Princess Leia calls Han Solo a 'stuck-up, half-witted, scruffy-looking nerf herder'.

BEYOND BUFFY: ANGEL AND THE EXTENDED BUFFYVERSE

The number of spin-offs, rip-offs, take-offs and other kinds of -offs on *Buffy* is bewilderingly vast, and beyond ready mapping. Here is a quick primer of some of the more conspicuous developments.

Angel

The major dramatic spin-off from *Buffy* to date has been the action series *Angel*, broadcast in 110 episodes, across five seasons from October 1999 to May 2004 – at which point it was cancelled as a result of dwindling audience figures. In its third and fourth seasons, though, it sometimes outperformed its progenitor show in the ratings. (*Buffy*, by the way, usually managed to pull in audiences of between four to six million in the USA on its first screenings; not very large when compared to the big hit shows on ABC and the other major networks, but very healthy for a smaller channel like WB.)

Angel (played by David Boreanaz) was a major supporting character in the first three seasons of *Buffy*; the character left the show at the end of Season Three, after a metaphysically catastrophic love affair with Buffy herself. In terms of the show's mythology, Angel was born in eighteenth-century Ireland, and was turned into a soulless vampire – the dreaded Angelus – while still young. He cut a destructive swathe amongst humankind for years, until a gypsy cursed him by restoring his soul, meaning that he was suddenly flooded with unbearable remorse for all his evil actions. The curse eventually set him off on a long path of redemption, which lead him – via his eventful stay in Buffy's town, Sunnydale – to Los Angeles, where he sets up as a private investigator, much in the Philip Marlowe mould, save that his bad guys are mainly supernatural.

Angel had a slightly darker tone than most *Buffy* episodes, tended to have less comedy and love interest, was mildly more adult, and definitely more calculated to appeal to a predominantly male audience: Whedon called it a 'guy's show'. Even so, a fair part of *Buffy*'s loyal fan base tuned in, too, especially once well-loved characters like Spike began to show up in cameo roles. Where *Buffy* was, as Whedon often put it, a sort of horror film set in a high school, Angel self-consciously referred back to the classic days of *film noir*, both in its sense of Los Angeles as a place where the bright sunlight failed to penetrate a deeper moral darkness, and in its taking a flawed, potentially unreliable man as its protagonist. Angel's suppressed vampirism, as one of the show's producers said, is in the nature of an alcoholism or addiction metaphor: one glass, one shot, or in his case one bloody bite, and he's doomed again.

After *Angel* was cancelled, Whedon continued to follow the characters' exploits in a series of comic books. (Spike, as noted, has also had his own series.)

Buffy on the Page

For the benefit of all those thousands and thousands of fans who soon found that a weekly dose of *Buffy* on television was simply not sufficient, Joss Whedon has created, commissioned, or permitted many related ventures into other media:

✝ Since 1998, Pocket Books have published more than sixty tie-in *Buffy* novels.

✝ Since the same year, Dark Horse publishers have been publishing comics about the adventures of Buffy.

✝ In 2003, Whedon scripted *Fray*, an eight-part comic about the adventures of a young female Slayer in the distant future.

✝ In 2004, he scripted *Tales of the Vampires*, another comic series.

And, since March 2007, he has been writing a set of comics entitled *Buffy the Vampire Slayer: Series Eight*, which picks up where the 'canonical' Series Seven left off, and shows what would have happened to Buffy and the surviving Scoobies had the show not been cancelled. Whedon has stated that *Series Eight* will eventually run to forty issues.

Miscellany

It would be madness to attempt a list of all the video games, role-playing games, DVDs, CDs, T-shirts and other merchandising spawned by Buffy; and folly to chart the show's fortunes among fan groups, on the Internet (it was one of the earliest television programmes to inspire whole Internet communities), or in academic circles, where *Buffy* studies refuse to lie still, and continue to proliferate at an alarming rate. There have been many plans for further film and television ventures, including a film featuring Spike, and *Ripper*, a drama about the unexpectedly wicked early years of Rupert Giles, Buffy's mentor. Other plans, or in some cases just feverish Internet-driven rumours, include a vehicle for the character Willow, a series provisionally entitled *Slayer School* . . . and much else besides. The only safe prediction is that Buffy and her Buffyverse are going to be part of popular culture for many years to come. You can stake a vampire, but a Slayer goes on and on.

DIME-STORE DRACULAS, ACT THREE: OF BATS AND BAT-MEN

With the increasing sophistication and popularity of comics over the last couple of decades, it is no surprise that vampires have been recruited in large numbers, both in conventional horror tales and in hybrid tales, where they play their part in war stories, crime stories, pirate yarns, satires, and good, old-fashioned superhero fare. In the last instance, one of the most notable graphic novels of recent years brought together two types of bat-men.

Batman and Dracula: Red Rain. Sooner or later, the idea was bound to have occurred to someone: Batman, a creature of the night, should come into conflict with *nosferatu* . . . and then, in an ugly twist, be bitten and become a bloodsucker in his own right. (Note, too, the full-length animated feature *Batman vs. Dracula* (2005), partly inspired by the *Red Rain* comic, in which Dracula, not without justice, points out that the Batman's legend is a variant of his own.) This starts out as conventional superhero stuff of good versus evil, then, once Batman becomes infected and mutates, grows darker and darker. In the end, the bat-creature is little more than claws, wings and fangs. Created by Doug Moench, Kelley Jones and Malcolm Jones III, the tale was continued in two sequels, *Bloodstorm* and *Crimson Mist*; the trilogy was collected in book form as *Tales of the Multiverse: Batman-Vampire* (2007).

Preacher. Proinsias Cassidy, an Irish vampire, is a major secondary character in this popular DC/Vertigo series, written and drawn by Garth Ennis and Steve Dillon. Cassidy, born in 1900, fought against the British in 1916 and was attacked by a bog monster of some kind in the same week as the Easter Rising. Suffering from symptoms he does not understand, Cassidy makes his way to New York, where he stumbles across a copy of *Dracula* and finally works out what has happened to him.

Dracula vs. King Arthur. This hardly requires explanation, at least as a plot premise.

Bite Club. A lavish and often clever contemporary tale of gangsters and fangs, with a Florida setting, a good deal of R-rated sexual goings-on, and one interestingly tormented character: a vampire priest.

The League of Extraordinary Gentlemen. Mina Harker, from *Dracula*, has become a (good) vampire and joined forces with the likes of Captain Nemo and the Invisible Man to combat evil-doers. Written by the unequalled genius of the comics field, Alan Moore, and made into a disappointing film.

30 Days of Night. A good premise: Barrow, a remote town in Northern

Alaska, is starved of daylight for a whole month each winter. (In this comic, anyway. The real Barrow has sixty-seven days of darkness, but that doesn't sound as catchy.) One winter, a pack of bloodsuckers moves in, to feast without fear of the coming dawn . . . This graphic novel was immensely successful, and generated several sequels, as well as a feature film (see below).

Sea of Blood. Vampires at loose on the High Seas! Aaaaarrrrh! In fact, vampirates! (Note that vampiracy is also the subject of a thriving sub-genre of contemporary children's fiction.)

From the Land of the Setting Sun: Vampire Manga and Anime

The universe of manga – Japanese comic books – and their animated counterpart, anime, is vast beyond ready reckoning. It encompasses just about every narrative genre from fantasy to hard-bitten realism, and vampire stories thrive within its bounds. Here are five of the best-known, best-selling vampire manga:

Hellsing (artist: Kohta Hirano). Set in a fanciful version of the United Kingdom, *Hellsing* follows the adventures of a group known as the Holy Order of Protestant Knights, a body sworn to defend Queen and Country against the Nazis, the Catholic Church and other forces of evil. (Don't shoot the messenger, I'm just reporting the facts.) In each generation, the head of the HOPK is the latest descendant of the bloodline of Abraham Van Helsing; as the series begins, this is Sir Integra Fairbrook Wingates Hellsing (sic). The group's secret weapon is Alucard, a powerful, 600-year-old vampire.

Vampire Hunter D (author: Hideyuki Kikuchi; artist: Saiko Takaki). In a future, post-apocalyptic world, vampires triumphantly rule the earth. But, slowly, humans are emerging from the ruins and fighting back. Into this bitter conflict comes 'D' – a half-human, half-vampire 'dhampir', possessed of all the skills, strength and savvy he needs to survive, as well as a startling beauty that makes him irresistible to vampires.

Chibi Vampire (artist: Yuna Kagesaki). Young Karin is the misfit in her family of vampires; she is a vampire in reverse. Once a month, she suffers from a surfeit of blood, and has to pass it on to a human. Anyone who receives this special blood becomes super-charged with vitality, optimism and well-being. Oh, the shame.

Vampire Knight (artist: Matsuri Hino). The Cross Academy has a secret identity. By day, it is just an ordinary school; but by night, it becomes a training centre for aristocratic vampires. The adopted daughter of the academy's president, Yuki, is in peril when she stumbles across the secret; and her life is complicated still further when she becomes caught up in a love triangle.

Rosario+Vampire (artist: Akihisa Ikeda). Another tale of a secret academy. Yokai, a rebellious lad, is kicked out of all normal schools and so is forced to enrol at the Yokai Academy. Alas, 'yokai' means 'monsters'. At first, things don't seem too bad: a pretty girl called Moka appears to have a crush on him. But does she love him for himself, or just for his nice plump arteries?

Other prominent vampire manga include: *Blood +; Canon; Castlevania, Curse of Darkness; Lament of the Lamb; Millennium Snow; Model; The Record of a Fallen Vampire; The Reformed; Trinity Blood; Vampire Kisses; Vassalord*. A galaxy awaits you.

Sayonara!

UNDEADING IT UP AT THE HOTEL TRANSLYVANIA: VAMPIRE WEEKENDS

The acronym LARP means 'Live Action Role Playing', and designates all those activities which involve dressing up as characters and playing out shifting plotlines, usually on weekend breaks at obliging hotels. (For an account of what these occasions feel like for a newcomer, see Paul Bibeau's light-hearted book *Sundays With Vlad*, 2007.) There are dozens and dozens of vampire LARP games, including some based on Anne Rice's novels; one of the most popular has been *Vampire: The Masquerade*, written by Mark Rein-Hagen and first published in 1991. *VTM* incorporates an intricate mythology-cum-history, which proposes that in 1435, the Inquisition started to hunt down and destroy all descendants of 'Caine' – vampires, known as 'the Kindred'. In 1486, an international convention of the undead formulated a law of survival: from now on, all vampires would follow the Masquerade, and spread the word that vampirism is a thing of myth.

This worked for a long time, but in the twentieth century, the rise of New Age cults, psychedelic drugs and so on helped to undermine this useful scepticism; so vampires are now in increasing danger of being 'outed', as it were . . . As you might expect, the overall mythology is a great deal more complicated than this introduction suggests. The game inspired a short-lived American television series, *Kindred: The Embraced*, in 1996.

CARPENTER'S GOTHIC

Throughout the 1970s and early 1980s, the name of John Carpenter was synonymous with low-budget, high-polish thrillers, horror stories and science fiction, often seasoned with plenty of iconoclastic wit. Just reeling off the titles can bring pleasure to movie buffs of a certain age: *Dark Star, Assault on Precinct 13, Halloween, The Fog* . . .

Great stuff. If only Carpenter had turned to vampire themes when he was on a roll. His later output, alas, is violently unpredictable, with an occasional eccentric gem here and there (*In the Mouth of Madness*, though it fared poorly at the box office, may be the cinema's best treatment of H. P. Lovecraft's mythology to date), but also several duds and misfires. His name was still enough of a selling point by the late 1990s, though, that it made sense to call his first undead adventure *John Carpenter's Vampires* (1999).

The film proved to be . . . all right. Not bad. Even quite cool, at times. It plays, like the third *Dusk Till Dawn* feature, somewhat in the manner of a Sergio Leone spaghetti western, and stars the ever-reliable, ever-creepy James Woods as Jack Crow, a lean-limbed, foul-mouthed, ornery vampire slayer in shades and leather jacket, whose favourite tool is a bit like Captain Ahab's: he locates the vampire in its safe-house, fires a harpoon at it, and winches it out into the sunshine, where it burns to death. The team-work and camaraderie of Crow's team is also reminiscent of the male groups in classic films by Howard Hawks – Carpenter's chief influence as a film-maker. The main plot is a revenge yarn: after the team has successfully taken out a 'nest' of 'goons' – the vampire hunters have their own slang – a Master Vampire tracks them down to the motel where they are carousing and whoring, and slaughters almost all of them. So Jack puts together a new team, which includes a prostitute (bitten, and obviously beginning to turn), a survivor of the first attack (bitten by the prostitute, so equally untrustworthy) and a priest, then sets off on the hunt.

Carpenter also lent his name to two sequels, of sorts: *Vampires: Los Muertos* (2002, directed by Tommy Lee Wallace, and starring Jon Bon Jovi as the vampire hunter), and *Vampires: The Turning* (2005, directed by Marty Weiss), a US/Thai co-production, heavy on the martial arts.

THE JUDAS KISS: TWENTY-FIRST CENTURY DRACULA

Dracula 2000 (2000, directed by Patrick Lussier and produced by Wes Craven; also known as *Dracula 2001* in the regions – including the UK – which didn't distribute it in time). This is chiefly memorable for a lurid late sequence which reveals that Dracula is actually – aha! – Judas Iscariot. The whole business about vampires being repelled by silver dates back, it seems, to that sordid deal with the thirty pieces of same, and Judas's subsequent suicide. Apart from a very, very brief prelude showing the *Demeter* at sea, and a longer one in modern-day London, which introduces Christopher Plummer as Van Helsing, the film is mainly set in and around New Orleans at Mardi Gras time. Gerald Butler plays Dracula with longish black hair and matching clothes, as if he were the lead singer of a metal band; he is supposedly irresistible to women, who eye him up at every possible occasion.

There were two straight-to-DVD sequels: *Dracula II: Ascension* (2003) and *Dracula III: Legacy* (2005), set in Romania. Different actors played the title roles.

THE NEW RED ARMY: POST-SOVIET VAMPIRES

Night Watch and *Day Watch* (2004 and 2006, both directed by Timur Bekmambetov). Freely adapted from a best-selling trilogy of novels by the Moscow-based author Sergei Lukyanenko: *The Night Watch* (Russian edition 1998; English translation 2006) and its sequels *The Day Watch* and *The Twilight Watch*. These first-rate fantasy epics are all about a centuries-old conflict between the Forces of Night and the Forces of Light, waged without the knowledge of humankind until two rogue vampires threaten to uncover the great secret and blow the whole thing wide open. The books have sold more than two million hardcover copies in Russia alone; the first two titles have been brought to the screen with great visual flair by the director Timur Bekmambetov. With his production team, the director worked wonders to overcome the constraints of a limited budget – estimated at the equivalent of about $4.5 million – and poor national production infrastructure, and to produce some really eye-popping, fast-moving hokum. Box office giants on their own territory, these were the first Russian productions to leap into Western multiplex cinemas, albeit in dubbed versions. Hollywood took notice, and recruited Bekmambetov to direct the blockbuster thriller *Wanted* (2008), starring Angelina Jolie. He is said to be at work on the last part of the trilogy, which is scheduled for release at the end of 2009.

DRACULA VS. WOLF MAN, REVISITED: THE UNDERWORLD SERIES

Underworld and *Underworld Evolution* (2003 and 2006, both directed by Len Wiseman): very much in the spirit of the *Blade* series, though their tone and visuals are generally darker. This flashy, expensive-looking production backs away from most of the traditional spooky pleasures of vampire fiction, and opts instead for high-velocity action, with lots of car chases, shoot-outs, explosions, athletic martial-arts-style fighting in the manner of *The Matrix*, stabbings, high-tech weaponry, special effects and general mayhem. Somewhere behind the sound and fury is yet another tale about a centuries-long war, this time between vampires and their sworn enemies, the Lycans – in other words, lycanthropes or werewolves. To the sewer-dwelling Lycan proletariat, it is humiliatingly obvious that the castle-dwelling, quasi-aristocratic vampires have long held the upper hand, but the Lycans are starting to fight back hard, and they have a number of secret advantages, including a new type of bullet that radiates ultraviolet rays: in effect, pellets of deadly daylight.

Kate Beckinsale stars (and is the primary attraction) as Selene, a vampire super-warrior and combat-hardened wolf-killer who sports a shiny, skin-tight leather body suit and, usually, a long black cloak.

When in full vampire mode, she also has a tasteful pair of white fangs and bright blue eyes. Selene is armed to the aforementioned fangs both with science-fiction style handguns – firing silver bullets, of course – and traditional ninja weapons. She is supernaturally fast and strong and can jump from the tops of high buildings, landing gracefully and harmlessly on her feet in a way that would make any self-respecting cat sick with envy. Way cool. (Ms Beckinsale opted not to take part in the prequel, *Underworld: Rise of the Lycans*, which opened in early 2009, to decent box office but dismissive reviews.)

Vampire fans are usually fairly snooty about the *Underworld* franchise, but it is not without merit; there is, for instance, a very enjoyable performance – albeit a performance that has to fight its way through hundreds of pounds of ghoulish make-up and a lot of blood-filled plastic tubes – from Bill Nighy as Victor, an ancient vampire leader who in the first film has to be raised from his slumbers a century or so early to intervene in the war; and also from Michael Sheen, feral and raging and hairy, a million miles away from his celebrated role as Tony Blair, in the form of a Lycan leader.

VAN DALISM

Van Helsing (2004, directed by Stephen Sommers). Kate Beckinsale stepped back into similar costume, but remained human, for this otherwise unrelated film, which, despite the best efforts of responsible film critics around the world, cleaned up at the box office and has been rated by the Internet Movie Database as the second highest-grossing vampire film of the last three decades. Her presence apart, this is a dim-witted and lamentable thing, clotted with overblown special effects and frenetic fight scenes, hopelessly wedded to the policy that the more gimmicks you shove up on screen, the better the results will be. It stars Hugh Jackman as the titular Van Helsing – not remotely like Stoker's original polymathic scholar Abraham Van Helsing, but a thick-eared, two-dimensional Indiana Jones-type, armed with a repeat-action crossbow and rechristened Gabriel Van Helsing. Cynics have suggested that this film was largely conceived as way of repackaging the classic movie monsters in which Universal hold copyrights, and, sure enough, all the old monsters are here: the Frankenstein creature, the Wolf Man . . . and Dracula. (Mr Hyde, doubling up as a kind of Hunchback of Notre Dame in an early sequence, also puts in an appearance.) If only, as was rumoured shortly after the release of Coppola's *Dracula* film, Anthony Hopkins had been persuaded back into the Abraham Van Helsing role for an adventure more in the spirit of Stoker's original.

POINTED TOES, POINTED TEETH: A NEW DANCE OF THE VAMPIRES

Dracula: Pages from a Virgin's Diary (2002, directed by Guy Maddin). Originally shot for screening on Canadian television, but given a theatrical release in response to widespread critical enthusiasm, this is a straightforward ballet version of the tale, performed by the Royal Winnipeg Ballet and filmed by the avant-garde Canadian director Guy Maddin. It may sound unpromising, but in fact is excellent; simply, one of the very best treatments of the Stoker theme, and – apart from relegating Harker's Transylvanian adventures to a swift flashback – on the whole reasonably faithful to the novel. It is shot silently, and in styles reminiscent of the silent cinema, though its standard black and white is varied from time to time with coloured filters and CGI effects. Zhang Wei-Qiang dances and acts the part of the Count; most of the score is derived from themes in Mahler's symphonies.

This is, at present, the most famous vampire ballet, but it is not the only one of its kind. According to David J. Skal, there were at least two such productions in the nineteenth century: *Morgano* (1857) by Paul Taglioni and J. Hertzel, and Rotta's *Il Vampiro* of 1861. In the twentieth century, Aaron Copland and Harold Clurman collaborated on *Grogh*

(1925), inspired by Murnau's *Nosferatu*, but it was never produced. A piece entitled *Vampaera*, originally with music by Debussy, was staged in Bristol by the Western Ballet Theatre (1956). More recently, Les Grands Ballets Canadiens mounted *Love, Dracula* by James Kudelka, and an American company produced a *Dracula* which followed Stoker's plot with a reasonable degree of faithfulness.

UN†IL †HE FA† LADY SCREAMS

Recently released on CD, the American opera *Nosferatu* was a collaboration in the late 1990s between the composer Alva Henderson and the well-known poet and cultural diplomat Dana Gioia (whose libretto for the work was published in 2001, with an interesting essay both on Murnau and on writing verse for music). It is a curious fact that *Dracula* has been adapted into a musical countless times, but has never served as the basis for a full-scale opera. To date, *Nosferatu* is the closest version we have.

IN SPACE, NO ONE CAN HEAR YOU BI†E

Dracula 3000 (2004, directed by Darrell Roodt): this is an ultra, ultra-low-budget science-fiction flick – it appears mainly to have been shot in a disused power station and the props look like they were bought at Woolworth's – which plunders in roughly equal measure from *Alien* and *Dracula*. Thus, the captain of a recovery vessel is called Van Helsing; his technical officer is called Holmwood; and his youngest crew member is Mina Murry (*sic*). While cruising in the Carpathian Galaxy (double *sic*), they encounter an abandoned vessel, the *Demeter*, drifting in the general direction of Earth. Once on board, they find that the vessel's skipper, dead these fifty years, has lashed himself to a control panel with a crucifix in his hands . . . You can probably guess the rest.

PLASMA SCREENS: VAMPIRES IN TELEVISION

John Mark's novel *Fangland* (2007) is a self-conscious replay of Stoker in both theme and structure, with emails and 'therapy journals' here taking the place of letters and telegrams. The Jonathan Harker figure is a woman – Evangeline Harker – an associate producer who works for the American current affairs programme *The Hour* (for which we can safely read *60 Minutes*, since Marks himself used to be a producer on that show). She is sent off to Romania to interview a man who is rumoured to be the head of organized crime in the region. But this strange fellow seems to live all alone in a big, empty, ruinous building – a former hotel – and when Evangeline, now in effect his prisoner, tries to film an interview with him, his image does not register on tape. And then this sinister Transylvanian makes his way to New York, and the offices of *The Hour* . . .

IN COLD BLOOD: ARCTIC VAMPIRES

30 Days of Night (2007, directed by David Slade). Originally a best-selling graphic novel in 2002 (see above), which spawned a number of sequels, this film version went straight to the top of the US box office, and did well internationally. Though it cuts out a fairly substantial subplot from its source, it otherwise remains close to its origins, and is a reasonably well-staged action thriller, marred primarily by scenes which are rather too obviously shot on sound stages (you rarely see breath condensing in the cold air). Josh Hartnett plays the hero Sheriff Oleson, who has to rally his fellow citizens of Barrow, Alaska when a tribe of hungry vampires moves in on the town during its annual month of complete darkness. One nice touch: the vampires speak their own language – it was devised for the film by a lecturer in linguistics – and have to be subtitled for the benefit of those who have never studied vampiric. At least two sequels are said to be in preparation.

DEAD BORING, DEAD BEAT

At last: someone has had the wit to conceive of the vampire as a downtrodden, over-worked loser. In the graphic novel *Life Sucks* (2008) – by Jessica Abel, Gabe Soria and Warren Pleece – Dave Miller is a kid stuck for all eternity in his late teens, and compelled to work night shifts at a convenience store, The Last Stop. Dave originally came here a couple of years earlier, when his blood was still warm, looking for a job; the owner, 'Radu' from Romania, took him into the back room, and, well . . ."

BLEEDING HEARTS: ROMANTIC VAMPIRES

Many bookshops have recently developed a series of shelves devoted to what is sometimes called 'Paranormal Romance'. The UK chain Waterstone's, a touch more wittily, has a sign which reads 'The Lady and the Vamp'. This section of the bookshop is often at least equal in size to the traditional gut-wrenching, eye-gouging horror section usually frequented by male readers. The novels you will find here are pretty much all cross-breeds between two existing strains: romantic fiction and supernatural or vampire fiction. (Sometimes they feature werewolves or other kinds of shape-shifters, or reincarnated Greek gods, or demons, or what have you, but for the most part the supernatural villains and heroes that stalk or swagger through their pages are regular old *nosferatu*.) In one sense there is nothing new about these fictions; as we have seen, the sexiness of vampires has been one of their major attractions to the mass audience since the days of Byron, whose haughty features are usually not hard to discern in this type of product, no matter the name under which he travels.

As a publishing phenomenon, however, this sort of hybrid bodice-ripper and throat-piercer actually is a moderately new thing under the sun. Its obvious antecedents are Lugosi in the 1930s; *Dark Shadows* in the 1960s; the Frank Langella *Dracula* in the 1970s; Anne Rice's novels; and such sexy male *Buffy* characters as Spike and Angel. One other forerunner, not mentioned so far, is the prolific novelist Chelsea Quinn Yarbro (born 1942), who in her *Hotel Transylvania* (1978) introduced the dashing character of Saint-Germain (full name: Rakoczy, Comte de Saint-Germain), a one-time alchemist turned charming and erudite vampire, some 3,000 years old. Yarbo pursued Saint-Germain's exploits through a number of sequels:

✝ *The Palace* (1979).

✝ *Blood Games* (1980).

✝ *Path of the Eclipse* (1981).

✝ *Tempting Fate* (1982).

✝ *The Saint-Germain Chronicles* (1983).

Saint-Germain, immune to most of the menaces that usually see off his kind (garlic, crucifixes and the like), is a connoisseur of female beauty and enjoys many affairs with mortal women, though he cannot produce semen, and takes the blood of his conquests instead. He manages to walk around wherever he pleases by having the appropriate soil sewn up in his shoes; why didn't Dracula think of that?

The Lady and the Vamp genre seems to be growing almost weekly, and there is no room here for more than a few representative authors' names – all, by the way, female.

Linda Lael Miller. Formerly a writer of conventional romance novels, she was inspired by the success of Anne Rice's books among her own fan base to branch out. She created the character of Aidan Tremayne, a handsome young buck who at the age of twenty-two had been rendered undead by a female vampire from Atlantis. Tremayne crosses over to the New World and, in a couple of hundred years later, begins an affair with Neely Wallace, a woman who (according to an ambiguous prediction) will either save or damn him. Their tale was told in:

† *Forever and the Night* (1993).
† *For All Eternity* (1994).
† *Time Without End* (1995).
† *Tonight and Always* (1996).

The floodgates had opened. Legions of romantic vampires marched into the world's bookshops, and remain there to this day.

Laurell K. Hamilton, author of the 'Anita Blake: Vampire Hunter' series. This posits an alternative present-day United States in which vampires and werewolves have come out from the shadows of myth and superstition and become integrated – not without difficulty – into the everyday world. (There are now many, many authors who use this conceit or something very like it, including Charlaine Harris.) Her heroine, Anita Blake, is based in St Louis and is one tough cookie. Her adventures began in *Guilty Pleasures* (1993), and continue in:
† *The Laughing Corpse* (1994).
† *Circus of the Damned* (1995).
† *The Lunatic Café* (1996).
† *Bloody Bones* (1996).
† *The Killing Dance* (1997).
† *Burnt Offerings* (1998).

Charlaine Harris is the author of 'The Southern Vampire Mysteries', a highly successful series, some of which have recently been adapted into a well-received television series on the American channel HBO called *True Blood*. (It began screening in September 2008.) This series of novels, lighter and a degree or so wittier than some of their competitors, are about the adventures of a young waitress who can read minds, and becomes entangled not only with vampires but with werewolves, elves, and witches too.

But there are dozens of others. And – confident prediction: we can expect many, many more.

DOWN THESE MEAN STREETS A VAMP MUST GO

There have been any number of Vampire Private Detectives in recent years, but probably the most purely enjoyable of these creations is 'Joe Pitt': a tough, hard-drinking, plasma-drinking vampire shamus who operates as an independent outsider in a New York that has been carved up by various mutually hostile vampire families. Joe Pitt was introduced in the novel *Already Dead* (2005) and continued his adventures in *No Dominion* (2006). The title is an allusion to Dylan Thomas's refrain, 'And Death shall have no dominion,' which Joe Pitt sees as a 'Poem on the Subway' while on his way uptown.

SMORGASBLOOD: A SCANDINAVIAN VAMPIRE

Let the Right One In, a novel by John Ajvide Lindqvist, was first published in Swedish in 2004 and translated into English in 2007. It is a strange and remarkable novel, one of the very best vampire fictions of recent years, not least because it often dwells as much on real-life terrors and miseries – school bullies, rent boys, drug addicts, paedophiles – as on the supernatural. It begins with a wretched twelve-year-old boy called Oskar, who lives with his mother in a low-rent housing estate in the suburbs of Stockholm. Oskar is lonely, horribly bullied, and given to wetting himself in class; but things look up for him when he forms a friendship with an odd little girl, Eli, who moves into an adjacent flat with a much older man. Or not much older, as Eli turns out to be a 200-year-old vampire, and gradually helps Oskar fight back against his tormentors. The book has been justly praised, and made into a fine film by the Swedish director Thomas Alfredson (2008). It was cited in several 'Best of the Year' lists in 2008 and an English-language remake is set for 2010, with Matt Reeves as director.

FINAL CURTAIN (FOR NOW): THE TWILIGHT ZONE

The Champ of Vamps

The last stop on our tour is inevitable: the *Twilight* series of young adult novels, by Stephanie Meyer, and related phenomena. You may, perhaps, have heard of them?

The four novels are:

✝ *Twilight* (2005).
✝ *New Moon* (2006).
✝ *Eclipse* (2007).
✝ *Breaking Dawn* (2008).

They have been astonishingly successful. By the end of 2008, books by Stephanie Meyer had sold some 29.7 million copies in the USA alone (and by March 2009, as I write, another 2.3 million units have been shifted.) In that year, Stephanie Meyer became the world's top-selling author, with sales of:

✝ *Twilight:* 10.07 million.
✝ *New Moon:* 6.95 million.
✝ *Eclipse:* 5.03 million.
✝ *Breaking Dawn:* 6.23 million.

(Meyers's novel for adults, *The Host*, has also sold 1.46 million copies.)

The *Twilight* novels have so far been translated into 37 languages, and have sold an estimated 42 million copies worldwide.

Something is happening here.

Necking Without the Fangs

Let us begin with the novel that launched it all. Meyer has said that the basic story of *Twilight* came to her in a dream, one night in June 2003. (Born in 1973, she was thirty, and had little experience as a writer.) Worked up into a narrative which runs to more than 500 pages – and which, she says, was written with *Pride and Prejudice* firmly in mind – the finished novel is a tale told by Isabella 'Bella' Swan, an intelligent and (though she seems not fully aware of the fact) highly attractive seventeen-year-old. As the novel begins, Bella is about to move from Phoenix, Arizona to Forks, Washington. Her parents have long been divorced, and until now she has opted to live for most of the year with her mother, Renee, seeing her policeman father in Forks only on vacations. But Renee has recently taken up with a professional sportsman, a minor baseball player, and wants to accompany him on his tours. A considerate young lady, Bella decides that her mother needs some breathing space, even though she does not relish the thought of moving from a warm climate to a damp and wintry small town with few amenities.

Quite soon, Bella becomes aware of a handsome but aloof boy in her year, Edward Cullen. For no reason that she can fathom, he seems to spurn her angrily at first, but then, just as mysteriously, grows ever more charming and affectionate, and their romance begins to kindle. But there are warning signs: he seems to have superhuman strength and speed (he rescues her from a near-fatal car accident by whizzing in front of the menacing vehicle and blocking it); his close-knit family are widely distrusted by most of the locals, and thought of as, at the very least, weirdos – possibly incestuous weirdos at that; and her Native American friend Jacob starts dropping grim hints about the true identity of the Cullens.

As most readers will have long since guessed, even if not previously briefed, the family is in fact a posse of vampires – albeit polite, wealthy, well-meaning, self-styled 'vegetarian' vampires, who feast only on animal blood. Well, it takes all sorts. By now Bella is hopelessly smitten with Edward, and the course of true love finally appears to be running smoothly, if unconventionally. But then a gang of not-so-good vampires shows up, and, after a preliminary scuffle, determines to hunt Bella down and tear her apart. The chase is on . . . and I will not provide a spoiler. You may draw your own conclusions from the existence of three sequels.

What this brusque summary does not adequately convey is the aspect of the Bella–Edward affair that has drawn most critical attention: in a word, abstinence. Not only do Bella and Edward refrain from full intercourse; for quite a while, they don't even so much as kiss, cuddle or hold hands. In terms of the vampire mythology, this chastity is, Edward explains, a necessary condition of their relationship: if they Went Too Far, he might not be able to contain the raging hungers inside him, and would fang her like a good 'un. The metaphor is so blatant as barely to count as a metaphor. Suspicious older liberals have sniffed conservative propaganda here (more exactly, conservative religious propaganda; the author is well known to be a practising Mormon); if so, the propaganda has found an eager audience.

New Blood

Judging myself disqualified (too ancient, XY chromosomes) from further comment on the fundamental appeal of the series, I turned for help to a gifted critic of the rising generation: Miss Artemis Irvine, aged ten. She kindly provided this:

Twilight: an Informed View

Twilight is a mix of romance, action and fantasy. That is what got me hooked. At the time I was reading *Twilight* I was really into fantasy romances and was desperate for anything like that which wasn't *Harry Potter and the Half-Blood Prince* (in my opinion the most romantic book in the Harry Potter series). I also like the book's main idea: Bella meets mesmerizing Edward, they fall in love, but he and his family turn out to be a vampires. As well as being fantasy and romance, Twilight succeeds in being rather comical. For instance I know that my friend (who has also read the series) and I find strange little Alice, Edward's vampire sister, funny when she insists on using Bella as a dolly, doing her hair and dressing her up. When Bella has had enough Alice complains that she can't remember her own human experiences of pampering. As Edward puts it, 'How can someone so tiny be so annoying?!'

My favourite thing about *Twilight* would be how impossible it all is, but how real it seems when you read it. I spent my entire Friday afternoon the day it arrived reading it, sinking deeper and deeper into the book, only to be interrupted by my mum for supper, during which I tried to explain to her how amazing I thought it was. Like the creator of *Buffy the Vampire Slayer*, Stephanie Meyer has set her story in high school, so not only has *Twilight* the thrills of vampires, werewolves and romance, but normal life activities such as school work, making new friends and going to the prom.

As the hero of the story, Edward is not only super strong and super fast like a real superhero, but adoring, patient and incredibly protective of Bella. No wonder she falls in love with him.

I feel on slightly surer ground when it comes to the movie version.

Fleshing It Out

The film adaptation of *Twilight*, released at the end of 2008, fully lived up to expectations, and rapidly became the best-selling vampire film of the last thirty years (which means: ever). Apart from some necessary and, on the whole, welcome trimming, and a few essential dramatic changes (Bella's email conversations with her mother become phone calls), it remains close enough to its well-loved source material to keep most fans happy and, for adults, is in many ways more satisfying. In place of Meyer's rather clunky prose – or, to be fair, Bella's clunky prose – there is the sombre, paradoxically lush cinematography, heavily biased towards blues, greys and dark greens; in place of the minutiae of high-school power games (off-putting, or at any rate dull for most adult readers), a fairly streamlined and compelling romantic narrative, which appeals as much to adult viewers as to teenagers.

Fluently directed by Catherine Hardwicke, from a screenplay by Melissa Rosenberg, it is done with almost entire sincerity and barely a hint of camp – only the special effects sequences are likely to provoke inappropriate titters. (Especially in the scenes in which vampiric skin twinkles in the sunlight as if sprinkled with glitter.) Robert Pattinson plays Edward (in his early twenties, the actor looks a lot more than seventeen, though a lot less than the ninetey-odd years that Edward has actually lived); Kristen Stewart is a suitably downbeat and introverted Bella. It may not be everyone's cup of plasma, but it is decidedly a superior piece of work; at the very least professional, at best not too far from poetic. It would be interesting to know the response of Stephen King, who has unkindly declared that 'Stephanie Meyer can't write a darn'. Tarnation!

Back to the Root (Canal)

For all that it has obviously risen from the fertile fields of 'Paranormal Romance', *Twilight* has had such a large and unprecedented impact on the mainstream culture – drawing in a vast audience that would usually shun vampires as a vampire shuns garlic – that one can already say that it has opened a new phase in the history of the genre. It may be that, a hundred years from now – if anyone is left to care about such things – Meyer will be neck and neck with Stoker as the most influential of all vampire novelists. (The film version of *New Moon* is already in pre-production: Chris Weitz will direct.) Quite where it will lead us is uncertain, though not beyond all conjecture. For the time being, we can say that one place it has already taken us is right back to the Romantics. Let us simply consider some of the qualities which make Bella – and the countless young girls for whom she is a surrogate – swoon for Edward.

Edward is:

☩ Handsome.

☩ Aloof, arrogant and disdainful.

☩ An outsider or outcast.

☩ Aristocratic (well, of old blood and refined tastes).

☩ Mysterious.

☩ Hiding a guilty secret or crime.

☩ Possibly cursed.

☩ Dangerous, in a seductive way.

Does this sound familiar? It should do: it is, almost item by item, the old recipe for a Byronic hero.

This is where we came in; and from whence, for now, we must depart.

THE SHAPE OF
FANGS TO COME

At the time of writing (March 2009), the following major vampire projects have been announced, or are in progress:

✝ Guillermo del Toro, the director of *Cronos* and *Blade II*, has signed a three-book deal with HarperCollins to co-write a trilogy of modern-day vampire novels, with the thriller writer Chuck Hogan. The first volume, entitled *The Strain*, is set for release in the summer of 2009.

✝ Justin Cronin has signed a book deal, and a tie-in film deal of $1.7 million, to write a similar trilogy, *The Passage*, about a vampiric plague that results from medical research gone wrong.

✝ Dacre Stoker, the great-grandnephew of Bram Stoker, has been commissioned (despite no known skills as a writer; he has been an Olympic pentathlon coach) as co-author of *Dracula: The Un-Dead*, an 'official' sequel, set in the year 1912. Again, there will be a film.

✝ Alex Proyas, director of *The Crow* and *Dark City*, is planning to make a film entitled *Dracula: Year Zero*.

✝ *New Moon*, the sequel to *Twilight*, is in pre-production. It is highly unlikely that *Eclipse* and *Breaking Dawn* will not also be filmed.

✝ *Twilight Watch*, the third part of Timur Bekmambetov's acclaimed trilogy of vampire epics, should be ready for release by the end of 2009.

✝ *Fangland*, the novel by John Marks, is being developed as a feature film for 2010 or 2011.

✝ Mary Harron is directing a film based on the vampire novel *The Moth Diaries*.

✝ Kim Newman has almost completed *Johnny Alucard,* his latest book in the *Anno Dracula* series.

A safe prediction:

There will be blood . . .

Acknowledgements

This book would have been a far more pallid thing without the friendship and generosity over the years of its two dedicatees, Anne Billson and Kim Newman. I am greatly in debt to both of them for many enjoyable conversations, lent books and videos, and general vampiric wisdom. (If you enjoyed this book, please buy theirs.) It is also a pleasure to acknowledge twenty-five years of educative friendship with Professor Sir Christopher Frayling, the Van Helsing *de nos jours*, and especially for the wide-ranging talks we have had in the South Kensington restaurant where some of *Curse of the Werewolf* was filmed.

Quite a few sections of the book were inspired by the activities of the legendary Sidney Vampire Seminar, in Cambridge; I'd particularly like to thank Anne Leone, President and Dante scholar; Louise Woods, Shakespearean and Terpsichorean; and Holly O'Neill, budding novelist, who converted me to *Buffy* fandom. Thanks, too, to our guest speakers: David Pirie (on Hammer films), Matt Thorne (on *Dark Shadows*), Peter Swaab (on Dreyer).

Additional grateful nods to: David Thompson for tracking down obscure DVDs, Martin Wallen for decades of shared vampire musings and for his enthusiastic advocacy of *Slave of my Thirst*, Alastair Brotchie for the rare copy of H. C. Artman's *Dracula Dracula*, Ben Moor for sharing his extraordinary knowledge of comics and for lending me *Bite Club* and other key titles, Anthony Wall for putting me on to Pierre Kast's *The Vampires of Alfama*, Laura Howell for *Count Duckula* and assorted manga discussions, Hunt Emerson for his Bram Stoker cartoon, Nick Lezard for informing me about 'Devlin Waugh' (shame that Waugh didn't make the final cut), John Baxter for esoteric film references, Marina Warner for her incomparable knowledge of folklore and Lisa Williams for nurturing my vampire screenplay-in-progress, *Red Dusk*. Rebecca Summers of the London Vampyre Group was gracious enough to allow me to become a neophyte member: I look forward to further adventures. Once again, Ron and Michèle Royal kindly allowed me to stay for a few months in their house on the coast of Maine, where most of *Bite* was written.

My gratitude to Philip Gwyn Jones antedates this project by many years; I owe him, as they say, Big Time. The brilliant Laura Barber of Portobello Books is the kind of editor authors dream about but seldom meet. Her encouraging, and discouraging, and often howlingly funny editorial emails made the task of writing more like play than work. I don't even begrudge the fact that she cut almost all my Latin phrases. *Gratias ago*.

Finally, my long-suffering wife Claire deserves sincere thanks for exceptional feats of patience. She thinks vampires are boring and ridiculous.

INDEX

LIBRARIES INVERCLYDE

To find out more about our books, to meet our authors, to discover new writing, to get inspiration for your book group, to read exclusive on-line interviews, blogs and comment, and to sign up for our newsletter, visit **www.portobellobooks.com**

encouraging voices,
supporting writers,
challenging readers

Portobello
BOOKS